Who Cares?

THE STORY OF BELFAST CITY MISSION

AMBASSADOR

BELFAST, NORTHERN IRELAND
GREENVILLE, USA

Who Cares?

THE STORY OF BELFAST CITY MISSION

NOEL DAVIDSON

AMBASSADOR

BELFAST, NORTHERN IRELAND
GREENVILLE, USA

Who Cares?
© Copyright 2002 Noel Davidson

ISBN 1 84030 130 9

Ambassador Publications
a division of
Ambassador Productions Ltd.
Providence House
Ardenlee Street,
Belfast,
BT6 8QJ
Northern Ireland
www.ambassador-productions.com

Emerald House
427 Wade Hampton Blvd.
Greenville
SC 29609, USA
www.emeraldhouse.com

CONTENTS

FOREWORD
by the President

It is a pleasure for me to write the foreword to this history of the Belfast City Mission, which has coincided most appropriately with the 175th anniversary, celebrated this year.

As a young man I was invited to join the Board of Superintendents in 1964 and in the last thirty-eight years I have been constantly encouraged by the witness of the many Christian workers who devote their time and talents to the proclamation of the Gospel of Jesus Christ. I am indebted to the missionaries, the Executive secretary, the office staff, all my fellow-office bearers and my predecessor as President, Professor D. A. D. Montgomery.

All of us, and I include all prospective readers of this excellent book, will join in expressing our thanks to Dr. Noel Davidson for undertaking to write it. With the guidance of God he has provided us with a fascinating history that should motivate us to praise our gracious Heavenly Father for all His wondrous works. May the reading of it enable us to both appreciate our debt to the past and prepare for the continuance of God's work in the future, in His will.

The spiritual needs of our city and province are as great today as they were in 1827 and we often wonder with the apostle Paul, 'Who

is sufficient for these things?'
The man who asks the question, provides the answer in the next
chapter of 2 Corinthians.

'Our sufficiency is of God,' he reminds us confidently.

Like the prophet Habakkuk, we are able to rejoice in our Lord
and in our salvation. We look up to the One seated at God's right
hand, the One whom we must continue to honour and present, as
His servants in the Belfast City Mission have been doing for one
hundred and seventy-five years.

'That in all things He might have the pre-eminence.' Col.1:18.

DESMOND J. SHAW
October, 2002.

INTRODUCTION

Back in the days when anyone travelling into Belfast came by stagecoach, and a man could have a shave and haircut for threepence, a group of Christian men became concerned about the social and spiritual state of the poor of the town. Anxious to do something about this they formed an organisation which they called the Belfast Town Mission, and appointed William Cochrane, a handloom weaver from Lisburn, as their first 'agent.'

Further agents were appointed to visit the homes of poverty-stricken people who inhabited the squalid courts and entries of the town, and preach the Gospel of light and hope in easily accessible 'stations'.

Then, through days of famine and hardship, and through days of economic advance and spiritual revival, the work kept on expanding.

When Belfast became a city in 1888, the Town Mission became the City Mission, and still the growth went on. The Mission has continued to work quietly and effectively in the city, adapting to the needs of the different generations, right up until the present day.

Whatever the age of the people being addressed, or the method of approach being employed, one thing has never changed. That is the aim of the Mission, which is to see men, women, boys and girls led to Christ for salvation.

When I was approached to write a book outlining something of the history of this witness for God for nearly two centuries, my initial reaction was that it would present me with quite a challenge.

How, or where, for instance, was I going to resource all the material needed for such a volume?

How, too, could I make it interesting?

Nobody wants a handbook of spiritual statistics in their Christmas stocking.

The question of finding background material didn't prove a problem at all, when I looked into it. The founding fathers of the Mission had been meticulous in their record keeping and detailed reports of the work in the early days were readily available. Then when I came to research the activities of the Mission in the last fifty years, I was able to contact both men and women who had been involved in the work, on the ground, in the city. Soon I had more information than I was ever going to need. There were files, reports, articles, booklets and newspaper-cuttings all over my study!

At this point I must digress to make a brief but sincere apology. If one of your relatives or close friends served God in the Mission for many years, and you can't find his name in this book, I'm sorry. As many as possible have been included, but if I had mentioned everybody the story would have run into ten volumes at least!

In an attempt to make this remarkable story as absorbing as possible I have endeavoured to combine three elements running in parallel throughout the book.

An account of what was happening in Belfast in the period under review helps keep the story in perspective, and an outline of the changes in the set-up and management of the Mission was considered essential. However, since people are mainly interested in people, the main theme of this book is the interaction between two different sets of individuals.

There are those dedicated children of God, the missionaries and their helpers, who set out to teach the truth of the Christian gospel, both by preaching and example. Then there are the others, the people whom they visited, spoke to, preached before, and taught in Sunday School. How did they react?

Halfway through this project I began to realise that I should be treating this piece of work not as a challenge, but a privilege. As I delved into the lives of men of God like William Maxwell and David Hamilton, to mention but two of dozens, I began to feel a sense of awe overcome me.

Who am I to be writing about such giants for God? I felt.

As I sat in a room one afternoon and heard two retired missionaries tell of their experiences, and the people they had seen led to Christ through persistent Christian care and witness, I felt painfully inadequate. It was an honour to be allowed to attempt to glean pertinent information from such humble, gentle, godly men.

In conclusion I would like to thank all the current staff of the Belfast City Mission for their support and assistance in the compilation of this volume. Sandra and Angela in the Mission office have been very patient in dealing with my many phone calls. The missionaries, too, some of whom I have had to call at home to verify minute details, have been extremely helpful to me.

I would like to mention three people in particular, though, for these men personify the entire thrust and vision of the Mission.

The first of these is Rev. Jackson Buick, M.B.E., the Honorary Secretary who has acted as an honorary research assistant to me for the past three months or so.

The others are the Executive Secretary, George Ferguson and his assistant, Robin Fairbairn. These servants of God and progressive agents of the Mission helped me in a multitude of ways, providing source material, arranging interviews, answering questions.

In all three of the above Christian gentlemen I found a profound underlying godliness and fervour for evangelism combined with a very practical knowledge of business and social constraints. 'Sanctified common sense', my father used to call it.

This is a story that covers one hundred and seventy five years of fruitful labour for the Lord on the streets and in the Mission Halls of Belfast. Thousands of the citizens of the 'capital of the North' have committed their lives to Christ as a result of this work.

If you are a Christian it is my prayer that your heart will be as thrilled to read of the blessing of God upon this Mission, as mine has been to write about it.

If you are not, may you be led to trust the Saviour as you read.

NOEL DAVIDSON
November 2002

1

UP FROM THE COUNTRY

Belfast had not attained the coveted city status, but was an expanding town with a rapidly increasing population when William Cochrane went to work there in the late 1820's.

Many others, who like himself had been cottage handloom weavers, were flocking into the town to try and earn something resembling a living wage. Such desperate people were prepared to work long hours in the fifty or more cotton mills whose tall black chimneys belched black smoke out across the skyline. This latest young man up from the country hadn't come to seek employment in some clattering cotton mill, though. He had come to work amongst the usually overcrowded and often squalid homes of the poor of the town.

Some years before, Rev. James Morgan had been visiting in the home of widow Cochrane outside Lisburn, and discovered that she had two sons and a daughter. The fatherless family seemed incredibly poor, and the two sons were trying to eke a living for all four of them by weaving linen on their handloom in a dark back room.

James Morgan found himself strangely drawn to one of the sons, William, who was obviously an intelligent, but totally uneducated lad. Having taken a special and prayerful interest in this talented young weaver over a period of time, Rev. Morgan had the pleasure of leading him to faith in Christ.

In the spring of 1827 James Morgan received a letter from the founders of a new Mission group enquiring if he could recommend a man who would be both physically and spiritually equipped for a demanding job they were hoping to create.

The notion of forming a group or society to work amongst the poor of the town had originated with Rev. Reuben John Bryce, who was the Principal of Belfast Academy and held in high regard in the town. Rev. Bryce was more than merely a respected educationalist, however. He was a sincere Christian whose heart burned for all the children of Belfast who would possibly never have the chance of an education of any sort, and for their parents with whom they lived in the town's dark lanes and entries.

Life had become so pointless for these pathetic people. Juvenile delinquency was prevalent amongst the young, drunkenness amongst their parents. Most of them had never been to a place of worship in their lives and had never heard the good news of the Gospel of Jesus Christ.

Having voiced his deep concerns to a number of his Christian contemporaries R. J. Bryce found that many of them would support him in his proposal to establish a 'Society for the Religious Improvement of the poor of Belfast, and its neighbourhood'. It was decided that this Society, which held its first formal meeting in February 1827, would operate under the less cumbersome title of the Belfast Town Mission.

Before launching the mission its founders thought it wise to set down a few ground rules to govern its function and some practical ideas as to how it should address the problem of reaching the careless, churchless, Christless population of the town.

These stated that the Mission would endeavour to procure a number of places, described as 'stations', in various parts of the town. Religious services would be conducted by carefully chosen men of committed Christian faith and high moral standing, called 'agents', in these stations, 'on any part of the Sabbath, and on a convenient weekday evening'. Either the agent responsible for the station, or another especially appointed to assist him, would 'visit the poor in their homes to read the Holy Scriptures to them and converse with them plainly and affectionately on spiritual matters'. They were also, as part of their visit, to invite the adults to the places of meeting and to encourage them to send their children to 'Sabbath School'.

It was emphasised, too, that the Belfast Town Mission was to be totally undenominational in character; the only proviso being that its agents would be men of 'approved evangelical sentiments'.

When the mission founders came to appoint their first 'agent' they wrote to a number of experienced and esteemed evangelical ministers setting out their vision for the Mission and the spiritual and moral attributes they would expect to find in an 'agent'. As the letter invited the senior ministers to make suggestions of anyone they considered suitable to undertake such work, Rev. James Morgan responded without delay.

He knew the very person!

The man who would be ideally equipped in every way to become the Mission's first agent was weaving cloth on a handloom in a remote country cottage outside Lisburn!

William Cochrane was invited to attend for an interview with Rev. R.J. Bryce and some others and was immediately appointed.

It was in the summer of 1827 that William kissed his mother goodbye and set off for Belfast to take up his new appointment.

As he wandered up what he assumed to be the main thoroughfare of the town, called High Street, on his first full day in Belfast William was mesmerised. Such noise! So much clamour! And every low fronted shop with its tiny windowpanes and wares scattered out at its cluttered front seemed to offer an unbelievable variety of goods for sale.

A small wrinkled woman with a black shawl wrapped around her head sat on a stool and croaked every now and then, "Broad, black or white, twilled or plain, penny tape at a halfpenny a yard!"

He had to duck to avoid a low pole projecting from a barber's shop. This establishment had a sign in the window advertising 'Easy Shaving and Haircut, Threepence.'

William found that threading his way down High Street required constant vigilance for if he wasn't planning a pathway around the tin ware, earthenware, and bags of turf or potatoes at a shop front he was stepping aside to let teenage boys and young men hurry past with long black bags on their backs. He was later to discover that these 'baggies' as they were nicknamed, sold bags of coal direct from the ships anchored at Hanover Quay at the end of High Street to those in the town who could afford such luxuries.

In the midst of all this William saw a distinctively dressed figure approach him. It was the town crier in his multicoloured costume. His knee breeches were untied and flapped about his fattish legs. This singular character was very red in the face, whether from his exertions or some other unidentified malady William couldn't be quite sure. He suspected, nonetheless, that his problem was in some way related to the fact that he insisted on ringing his bell and shouting intermittently at the top of his voice something about a shipload of fresh herrings which had just arrived at Limekiln Dock.

As he made slow progress down towards the quays at the end of the street, William Cochrane's mind was in a whirl. There were so many people all around him. It was such a change from their isolated cottage in the country where he had often gone for days without seeing anybody outside his own immediate family.

The bustle all about him indicated that the people he was stepping aside to pass, or stepping aside to allow to pass in the High Street, were people who, although they would never confess to having plenty, were certainly not in poverty. They were the Belfast residents who had something to sell, money to buy, or were even wealthy enough to ride in the two seat, two horse, four wheeled post chaises which trundled past from time to time.

Although he would no doubt have to come in contact with these busy business people in the course of his everyday life, these were not the people amongst whom he had been specifically appointed to work.

William caught occasional glimpses of the really destitute inhabitants of the town when he stopped to peer down the narrow, sunless entries, courts and lanes off High Street. There was Quay

Lane, Wilson's Entry, Pottinger's Entry, Hamill Court and dozens more such unplanned collections of overcrowded houses.

He was no longer a handloom weaver. William Cochrane had come up from the country to become the first appointed 'agent' of the Belfast Town Mission, and thus he would probably be the first person to bring the message of the gospel of joy and peace in Jesus Christ to many of the town's impoverished population.

Some day soon he would begin a systematic visitation of all these cheerless courts and dingy entries.

What would he find?

2

THE CINDER PICKER

It was hard at first.

When William Cochrane began to call at the homes of the poor he was regarded with some suspicion. Many were afraid that he had come to peddle an extreme brand of religion. On establishing with the starving people that he was only interested in their personal welfare he gradually began to be accepted, then welcomed, into the homes.

Although times had often been difficult for his family outside Lisburn, they had never experienced anything like the abject misery that William was to discover in the lanes of Belfast. His simple country mind had never imagined that such poverty, both physical and spiritual, existed anywhere in the world.

On one of his initial visits to a cluster of what could only be described as hovels, he came upon a pathetic family. A woman, probably the mother, sat on a stool, which was the only item of furniture in a bare, damp room. Clustered around her in a semicircle on the uneven floor were three shivering children, clad only in rags. They were at dinner. This consisted of a few potatoes in an earthenware dish and a little salt on a piece of broken plate. That was all, and that was for four of them.

It was a pathetic situation, which for William became even more distressing when he began talking to them and found that none of them had ever heard of the love of God for the world, and for them.

One Friday afternoon he was making his first foray into a narrow entry in which there were a few dark houses.

When he knocked on the door of one dismal dwelling and a woman's voice invited him to enter he found the woman busy at her work. It was, though, an occupation which William had never seen before nor did he even realise that it existed.

The sole occupant of that dingy room was seated in the middle of the floor, surrounded by containers of various shapes and sizes. Her face, hands and patched and ragged clothing were caked with a grey-black grimy dust.

William was mystified by the strange set-up. "What are you doing there?" he enquired gently.

"I'm picking cinders," the woman replied. "I go out in the morning and collect them. Then I bring them home and clean them and sell them. It is the only way I can make a few pence to buy us a morsel of bread."

"Do you live alone?" William went on, touched by the sad situation. "Or is there anybody else in the house to help you?"

"No, there is nobody to help me," the forlorn cinder picker replied. "But my son is in the room at the back, sick," and she gave a sweep of a blackened arm, which peeped at intervals through the holes in a blackened sleeve. "I don't think it is the fever, mind you, though it has been through almost every family in the entry."

The agent stooped low at the lintel and entered the small back room. Having allowed his eyes to become accustomed to the gloom he found a lad lying on a heap of rags on the floor. He was asleep. Flies crawled all over his thin, pale face.

Reluctant to disturb him, William retraced his steps out past the woebegone mother, and towards the door and the only slightly less putrid air in the entry outside. His figure in the doorway blocked any light from the woman's face as he turned and said, "I would like to speak to your boy when he wakens up. I will make a few more calls and then come back before I leave the area."

On keeping his promise more than an hour later, William found the young man awake. He looked extremely ill. William hadn't been a year in his new job yet, but he knew enough to recognise a condition he had already seen a number of times before. The cinder picker's son was probably dying from consumption.

When he had introduced himself and spoken generally about the lad's weak physical condition, William steered the conversation towards spiritual issues. Upon asking permission to read the Scriptures he turned to Romans chapter five. Although aware that the sick boy's mother had also paused to listen to the reading, William decided to focus on verse eight, directing his attention towards the dying boy wrapped in rags on the floor.

He read the verse again, slowly. 'But God commendeth his love toward us, in that, while we were yet sinners, Christ died for us.' William then endeavoured to explain briefly the sinful nature of man, the love of God and the need for and value of the death of Christ. Neither the young man, who had obviously only a few more miserable days, or at the most, weeks, to live, nor his mother had ever heard that message before.

Before leaving the home William prayed for them both and as he was going out the door for the second time the mother begged him to return soon. She was so pleased that somebody had taken time to call and speak to them in their poverty-stricken plight. The socially aware and spiritually motivated agent for the Belfast Town Mission promised that he would. William Cochrane would have been planning to do so anyway, even without the mother's heartfelt plea.

As he gradually built up a relationship with some of the householders in the poorer areas of the town William began to establish a regular pattern of scripture reading in a few of the homes. He would invite a number of the residents from a lane or court to meet in one central house and he would read a Bible passage to them.

One afternoon he was just preparing to read to a small group of women in a house near the docks when a tall man in a sailor's uniform entered the room. He was a relative of one of the women and as he paced up and down the floor making smart comments his restless attitude had an unsettling effect on William's prospective audience.

"Would you care to sit down, sir?" William asked him, realising that it was high time he took control of the situation, otherwise the atmosphere would soon be anything but conducive to the reading of the Scriptures. "I am about to read the Word of God with these people and we would love you to stay."

"I haven't time," the sailor replied gruffly. "I'm just on my way out."

Having said that he made no effort to go out but continued to wisecrack with a couple of the younger women.

"Please sit down, sir," the agent begged again. "I am about to begin."

This time, somewhat to William's surprise, the sailor did take one of the two remaining seats and without giving him even the slightest chance to change his mind William commenced to read.

The sailor felt out of place and looked distinctly ill at ease at first, but as the reading proceeded he appeared to pay more attention. The Bible portion that William had planned to share with his group that day was Galatians chapters five and six.

When the catalogue of the works of the flesh was read out the sailor was suddenly captivated. They seemed to strike a note of recognition in his experience. Then as William continued with Paul's summary of the matter in the words, 'as I have also told you in times past, that they which do such things shall not inherit the kingdom of God', the sailor looked visibly moved and hit himself a punch on the thigh. The message was beginning to penetrate the careless and casual façade and prick the conscience lying just below.

William could discern that the Word of God was entering this man's heart and he continued to read on into chapter six. He was certain that he could see a tear glinting in the hardened sailor's eye as he read, 'Be not deceived; God is not mocked: for whatsoever a man soweth, that shall he also reap.' Acutely aware that to be seen weeping would not be in keeping with the macho man-of-the-world image he had been trying to present the sailor kept attempting to blink the tears away.

As was his custom, William prayed when he had finished a brief explanation of his reading, and then gave a tract to each person before they left for home. He had been careful to hand the visitor one entitled, 'The Prodigal Son'.

The big man looked down at the small scrap of paper nestling in his huge, rough hand. "That just answers me," he remarked, mightily subdued. "I have been a prodigal indeed." With that he made straight for the door and disappeared in the direction of the docks.

The agent of the Belfast Town Mission was left to wonder if he would ever see that seafarer again. Would he ever read the tract? Could he read? Would he ever repent of his sin and come to Christ?

Only God could answer those questions. All he could do was pray.

The seed had certainly been sown in fertile ground. Only God could make it grow.

The often tiresome work of house-to-house visitation was only one aspect of the work of the Belfast Town Mission in the early eighteen thirties. Another was the weekly meeting in the ever-increasing number of 'stations' across the town.

In less than four years five stations had been established. The first to be opened was in Brown Street in the heart of a densely populated neighbourhood. Within two years this Sunday evening sanctuary for the poor had become so popular that on summer evenings many were forced to sit outside in the court and listen through open doors and windows. To hear these people, many of whom had never been to church, singing hymns in the open-air was a great encouragement to the founders of the mission and its dedicated agents.

The second station to be opened was in Sandy Row on the Old Malone Road. This meetinghouse soon became so well attended that a larger building had to be acquired in the area to accommodate all who wished to come.

With so many having moved in from the country to settle in the Cromac Street area a station was established close to the New Market. The Sunday evening services there proved to be a haven for many Presbyterians who hadn't found a new place of worship in the town to which they had migrated in search of employment, and grew steadily as a result.

Two smaller stations, one in Lower Donegall Street and the other in Mill Row on the New Lodge Road were also greatly appreciated by the poorer residents of those districts.

This gratifying expansion of the mission meant that the organising committee felt the need to appoint two further agents. These were to help William with the arrangement of the meetings in the stations and the programme of visitation, which was widening in scope every week.

The renting of buildings and the employment of additional staff presented the committee with another problem, common to any organisation, and that was the need of funds. The poor people of the town, amongst whom they were so glad to be working, were struggling to stay alive, and so the necessary resources to continue the work had to be found elsewhere.

In an attempt to raise money to allow this valuable work to continue to develop, a number of the leading Presbyterian ministers of the day, including Rev. James Morgan and Rev. Henry Cooke, held special fund-raising services for the Mission.

The founders, committee and agents of the Belfast Town Mission were committed to doing everything in their power, and as guided by God, to address both the practical and spiritual needs of the poor of the town and God honoured that commitment. The necessary funds became available and the Mission continued to extend its work.

Before it, stretching out into the future, lay wonderful opportunities and no end of obstacles.

3

THE PASTOR OF THE POOR

In 1837 the mission suffered the loss of one of its most experienced and highly respected 'agents'.

William Cochrane, the godly man who had been the first person to carry the ministry of the mission into the back streets of Belfast, passed away. The man who had been so fresh, so strong, and so eager ten years earlier when he arrived in the town, and who had brought the message of spiritual healing and eternal hope into so many homes where fever was rampant, succumbed to the disease himself.

His loss was a big blow to the Mission and the Christian community in Belfast. In the ten years that he had laboured so unstintingly for the Lord his work had been of tremendous significance, both in establishing the Mission as a force for God and the Gospel in the town, and in seeing people come to know the Saviour, through his caring attention.

Rev. Dr. James Morgan, who had spotted his spiritual potential when he was still a handloom weaver in a remote country cottage, said of him, in a tribute after his death, 'William Cochrane was one of the mightiest instruments for good that Belfast ever saw. He was an eloquent man and mighty in the Scriptures. It is questionable whether any minister in Belfast was the means of more conversions than this agent of the Town Mission. Certainly among the poor no man ever had the same influence.'

Mr. William M 'Comb, the first secretary of the Mission, and obviously no mean poet, commemorated his passing with a poem. This work, written as a wholehearted commendation of the selfless service of William Cochrane also gives a real insight into the work carried out by the agents in those early days.

It is certainly worth quoting in full.

THE PASTOR OF THE POOR.

'He had the book of the law of the Lord with him, and went about and taught the people.' 2 Chronicles 17: 9

'Did not he weep for him that was in trouble? Was not his soul grieved for the poor?' Job 30: 5

The struggle's o'er and thou art gone
To where the weary find a rest;
Thy light that here so brightly shone,
Now brighter shines among the blest:
The Lord Jehovah was thy song,
Thy strength and thy salvation here;
And now, amidst a sainted throng,
Thy praises fill a higher sphere.

Where'er we go, whome'er we meet,
For thee the tears of sadness flow;
'The mourners go about the street,'
The rich in grief, the poor in woe!
The poor, now *rich* in faith and prayer,
The rich, in broken spirit *poor*,
Oft felt thy counsel and thy care,
Thy friendship and affection pure.

'Twas thine to break the fallow land,
That long had wild and barren lain,
To scatter, with a careful hand,
The seeds of thought, the goodly grain:
Now bending o'er the bed of death,
'Midst thick and pestilential air,
Oft weak in frame, but strong in faith,
Wrestling and prevalent in prayer.

Thou lov'dst the young with tender love,
Teaching their infant lips to praise,
And many a cherub now above,
With thee their hallelujahs raise.
Thou wert to weak decrepit age
A staff, a comfort, and a stay,
And ledst them from the sacred page
To Him, the life, the truth, the way.

The lonely widow blessed thy name,
The orphan clung around thy knee,
The outcast and the child of shame,
Found still a refuge-home in thee!
The drunkard, yes, that hopeless one,
Oft listened to thy warning strain,
And from his lips the cup he flung,
To lift it nevermore again.

Upright, benevolent, sincere,
Meek, unassuming, soothing, mild,
Thy sympathy oft dried a tear
That dimmed the eye of sorrow's child.
A burning zeal, by knowledge fanned,
A taste by holiness refined,
A feeling heart, a helping hand,
Were in thy character combined.

Farewell! Loved Pastor of the Poor!
Friend of my heart, a long farewell!
Thy hopes were bright, thy love was pure,
Thy faithfulness, Oh who can tell!
A 'polished shaft' in God's own hand,
A light now vanished from our eyes,
Too pure a flame on earth to stand,
Too bright to burn below the skies.

Dr. Morgan had lost the person he had often described as his 'right-hand man', William M 'Comb had lost the friend of his heart, and the poor had lost a most diligent pastor.

William Cochrane, though, first agent of the Belfast Town Mission, had left them all behind to enter into a rich reward.

4

ALL CHANGE FOR BELFAST!

On August 12, 1839, people from all over the town flocked to Great Victoria Street for a much-publicised event, which was to mark a significant phase in the development of Belfast. It was the opening of the Ulster Railway to Lisburn. Cheering, waving crowds lined the track to witness the coke-fired locomotive pulling its open carriages on the twenty-minute journey to its destination. Nearly three thousand people made the trip from Belfast to Lisburn and back on that first gala day.

Realizing that they were on to a winner the Ulster Railway Company extended its track through Lurgan to Portadown, and the North Eastern Railway to Ballymena, and the Belfast and County Down Railway were soon established. The railways grew apace. Tentacles of track began to creep stealthily farther and farther out across the northern half of Ireland, like spokes of a giant wheel. The stagecoach was soon to become a relic of the past.

The evolution of the railways coincided with one of the other most significant developments of the period. This was the transition from cotton to linen manufacture and the centring of the linen industry in the steam-powered mills of Belfast. The combination of these factors led to an even greater stream of poor weavers from the country flooding into the town in search of work. An almost daily increase in the population of the town led to an even greater workload for the extremely caring but already overstretched agents of the Mission.

There were six full time agents at work by the early 1840's. They and many of the leading ministers of the day were concerned at the introduction of what proved to be immensely popular cheap rail excursions on Sundays. This blatant desecration of the Sabbath, as they saw it, with its attendant evil of luring the weak-willed away from church, was yet another milestone of degeneracy against which they felt they must give battle in the struggle for the souls of men. One minister proclaimed that the railway companies were 'sending souls to the Devil at the rate of sixpence a day,' and that 'every blast of a railway whistle is answered by a shout in Hell'

The changes taking place in the town of Belfast were not totally confined to its social and economic structure either. The religious groupings in the town were in a state of flux as well.

In the decade before the coming of the railways the agents of the Belfast Town Mission had been successful in persuading many people to begin attending church services. At least partly as a result of their efforts eight new Presbyterian churches, among them Malone, Ballysillan, Berry Street and Newtownbreda, were opened under the control of the Synod of Ulster, and one in Alfred Place under the Secession Synod.

Then when negotiating committees from both synods reached an agreement on matters of doctrine and practice, they came together formally in Rosemary Street Church on July 10, 1840 and combined to form the General Assembly of the Presbyterian Church. This merger established the Presbyterian Church as a large and influential church grouping with four hundred and thirty-three congregations in its care.

While the negotiations that led to the establishment of the Presbyterian Church as we know it, were in progress, organisational difficulties and rumblings of denominational discontent had begun to surface within the Belfast Town Mission. It seemed that the Devil, not content with receiving souls from the railway company 'at the rate of sixpence a day', had decided to do all in his power to frustrate and thwart the efforts of those who were endeavouring to point other souls to Jesus, the one and only true Way to heaven.

The annual report of the Mission, presented by Mr. William McComb who had been its secretary since soon after it began, at the Annual Meeting in March 1940, showed that they had been coping admirably with the increasing number of challenges facing them in the rapidly expanding town of Belfast. The six agents had been making more home visits than ever, attendances at weekly meetings in the 'stations' had increased, some had come to know the Lord, and many adults up from the country had been encouraged to join their local churches and send their children to Sunday School. It appeared that the Mission was fulfilling its function, but then secretary McComb went on to say that they had a problem.

It was a big one, and it was an old one.

If they did not receive a substantial and virtually immediate financial fillip they would find it impossible to maintain the current level of staffing. Agents could not be supported and would have to be released.

This prospect appalled some of the ministers present, especially after the glowing report they had heard about the manner in which God was blessing their labours. Rev. David Hamilton made an impassioned speech expressing the belief that the Christian public would not allow the committee, for the sake of fifty pounds, to dismiss two of their agents who had done such valuable work amongst the poor. He went on to voice the opinion that the appointment of a great many more missionaries would do more for the peace of the town than all its police, jails and houses of correction combined.

Rev. Hamilton must have overestimated the ability of the plight of the poor to prick the conscience of the great 'Christian public' though, for they were not suddenly moved into donating massive amounts of money to the mission, and the inevitable occurred. By 1842 two agents had been forced to leave and seek other employment.

By then also the denominational differences which had been simmering in the depths for some time came up and burst forth on the surface causing disturbing ripples. These divisions, which manifested themselves in open disagreement on some matters, began to prove damaging to the image of the Mission.

Eventually a Church of Ireland member of the committee withdrew and formed another organisation to be called the Church Mission and administered solely by his church. This split was unfortunate in that it deprived the mission of its broadly interdenominational status, but by contrast there was plenty of work to be done amongst the poor of the town whose numbers were increasing at an alarming rate. If the recently established Church Mission could stretch out with practical help and the soul-emancipating message of the Gospel into hitherto unreached areas of the town, it could only be a blessing.

The withdrawal of Church of Ireland support left the former Town Mission almost totally under the control of the Presbyterian Church and thus they were left with little alternative but to reconstitute the Mission as an auxiliary organisation amongst the poor and needy.

Much discussion took place as to how and when this should be done and a meeting was eventually arranged for Monday October 9, 1843, in Rosemary Street Church. A number of the leading Presbyterian ministers of the day including Rev. Dr. Morgan, Rev. William Johnston, Rev. Thomas Toye, and Rev. Dr. Edgar aired their views on the subject.

It was decided that the Belfast Town Mission would be reconstituted as an outreach of the Presbyterian Church, though not officially affiliated to the General Assembly.

A number of new rules were proposed and adopted. These reflected the aim of making the Mission an even more effective organisation for the relief of distress amongst the poor and the advancement of the kingdom of God in the town.

Dr. Edgar proposed that ten men should be employed in addition to those already at work. The town was to be divided into districts with an agent responsible for visiting the people of that district, reading the scriptures with them and encouraging those not already attending a place of worship to join a local church.

Since it was now an arm of the Presbyterian Church it was proposed that more use should be made of licentiates and students for the ministry in the preaching of the Gospel in the various meetings of the Mission.

Although appearing sensible, some of the proposals, which had been agreed in principle, proved difficult to put into practice.

When the accounts were examined it was found, for example, that only two, and not the ideal ten, new agents could be employed, thus taking the number back to 1840 level. The preaching arrangements, too, turned out to be difficult to apply, for the licentiates were seldom available on Sundays as they were often responsible for conducting services in churches in various parts of the country. The students on the other hand were not always available for they had their studies to attend to, and so the bulk of the work, both of preaching and visitation, was carried on, as it always had been, by the lay agents of the Mission.

As the newly appointed agents, with their more experienced counterparts, settled into their designated districts, the work of the Mission continued to be blessed of God.

At an annual meeting held in May Street Church, which had, over the years become popularly known as 'Dr. Cooke's Church', in October 1845, Rev. William Johnston paid a glowing tribute to the work of the agents or 'missionaries'. He reported that seven communicants, who had been interviewed by him over the previous year, owed their conversion to God to the work and witness of two of the agents.

A note of caution was sounded by some of the speakers at that meeting, too, however. The droppings of blessing for which they were so justifiably grateful to God, were not in any way proportionate to the vast upward trend in the population of the town.

Little did they know, either, that a huge cloud of calamity was forming on the horizon, and was about to break, plunging all the inhabitants of the island of Ireland, but especially those in rural districts, into a deluge of abject misery.

There were desperate days ahead.

5

...AND I PERISH WITH HUNGER!

In the middle of September 1845 the maturing potato crop began to rot in the fields over much of the south and west of Ireland. Crops that had once appeared healthy were struck by blight. The tops withered and turned black and within a week the tubers, which had been almost ready for harvesting, were reduced to a soggy, slimy pulp. Many for whom potatoes were the staple, and in some cases the only food, faced starvation.

The full effect of this crop failure was not felt in Ulster, though, until the autumn of 1846 when the potato harvest failed over most of the island. By that time the plight of the people in the west was becoming increasingly grave. When haunting news of the widespread privations prevailing in many rural areas reached the town of Belfast, some of the committee members of the Belfast Town Mission decided to act. If the people of the country were starving, Christian charity, they felt, demanded that they endeavour to do something about it.

While the agents of the mission continued to visit the poor and destitute and conduct weekly meetings in their districts with untiring faithfulness, Rev. Dr. Edgar spent some time in the western province of Connaught during the summer of 1946. This visit made such an indelible impression on him that on his return to Belfast he wrote a pamphlet entitled, 'Cry from Connaught'. In this well-publicised paper he outlined in graphic detail the predicament of the people that he had witnessed. His description of a starving population, thousands of gaunt and emaciated men, women and children, with the look of impending death on their faces, or worse still, falling dead in their barren fields or joyless homes, proved heart-rending.

As has often been the case since early Christian times it was a number of the prominent ladies of the town who took the lead in practical charity. They formed themselves into the Belfast Ladies' Relief Association for Connaught, electing Rev. Dr. Edgar as their President. Inspired by the reports of distress and misery which seemed to increase both in frequency and frightfulness as the year laboured through a hungry autumn towards a starving autumn, these ladies went to work with a will.

As they made their collections and organised sales and events to raise funds, they were supported by William M'Comb who never missed an opportunity to mark the significant dates in the Christian calendar of the period with a poem. Although he had relinquished his post as secretary to the Belfast Town Mission before the reorganisation of 1843, Mr. M'Comb obviously maintained an active interest in the social and religious affairs of the town. On hearing of a bazaar organised by the ladies of the Relief Fund for Connaught he wrote this poem urging practical and financial support.

BAZAAR FOR THE FAMISHING POOR IN CONNAUGHT

There is wailing on the mountains,
Want in cottage, glen, and hill,
Broken pitchers by the fountains,
Present evil, threatened ill!

Bread there's none to buy or borrow,
Fathers, mothers, children cry!
Woman weeps the tears of sorrow,
Man the tears of agony!

Ye whom God hath blest with fullness
Hasten to the rescue soon;
Linger not with selfish coolness,
Help in time is double boon!

Many a needle has been plying
For our cause in many a home;
Come and buy, and save the dying;
Judgment, mercy bids you come.

The more affluent townspeople of Belfast, who up until then had escaped witnessing the worst of the famine, responded generously to such appeals and by the end of 1846 the Belfast Ladies' Relief Association for Connaught had raised between five and six thousand pounds. Their president undertook to oversee the distribution of these funds to the starving people of the west, regardless of religious or political affiliations.

"If we would act the part of the good Samaritan," he said, "it is enough for us to know that the cry of distress comes from a poor mortal like ourselves. Our first inquiry and our first anxiety must be how best to do him good."

Dr. Edgar continued to work for Famine Relief by extending his appeals to Great Britain and America. This led to the formation of the Belfast Relief Fund for Ireland and saw sixteen thousands pounds raised for the relief of the sorely afflicted.

Every penny that was raised was needed, for by Christmas 1846 the situation had become desperate. The total failure of the potato crop had sent many spinners and handloom weavers flocking from the country into Belfast. Their livelihood had been eroded over the previous decade, their staple food lay rotting in blighted, blackened heaps in the fields. It was, they reckoned, their only hope of survival.

If they couldn't find work in the linen mills, perhaps they could find employment in one of the new projects at the harbour. Belfast Harbour Commissioners had entered into contracts for the widening of the quays and the deepening of the channels to cope with an increase in shipping traffic, and this afforded employment for some.

Others who could afford it hoped to find a place on one of the many emigrant ships leaving that same harbour bound for Australia and North America.

Belfast, which had already a large number of poor and destitute struggling to hang on to life in its squalid lanes and entries found it difficult to accommodate the daily influx of hungry people from the country. A government official wrote at the time, 'in many of our back lanes and courts there are families in the most awful wretchedness, with scarcely enough rags to cover their shivering, emaciated bodies'.

That description could easily have been given of the situation that William Cochrane discovered when he came into Belfast to work for the Town Mission in 1827. The problem in late 1846, though, was that there were far more of these starving people in the streets, and their plight was worsening by the week.

The six agents of the Town Mission rose ably to the challenge that the change in the circumstances of so many presented to them. They moved from entry to court, from one dismal home to another dispensing help where they could. Despite the difficulties surrounding them in the city, these noble servants of the Lord also continued to conduct meetings in their appointed districts. These were welcomed by so many for whom poverty meant that they couldn't afford to 'dress up for church' on Sunday mornings, but who could attend the services of the mission on a Sunday evening in whatever few clothes they possessed. The warm welcome they received at those gatherings and the message of life and salvation proclaimed by the speakers brought both emotional solace and spiritual rest to a number of souls who were struggling to survive.

These agents of the mission were inspired to work tirelessly night and day amongst the physically weak and hungry and often spiritually indifferent of the town, not only by their personal commitment to God, but also by the selfless involvement of some of their leaders. Rev. William Johnston, no doubt shocked at some of the scenes he had heard described by the agents, and touched by some of the starving homes he had been called upon to visit, addressed a meeting in the Town Hall on 17 November 1846. This meeting had been called to arrange for the setting up of soup kitchens 'to grant a wholesome meal to those who were starving'. In thanking the provision merchants of Dock Ward for their donation of one hundred and ninety six pounds to the cause, Rev. Johnston told them that 'an unprecedented calamity has struck this country, and that, combined with the shortening of hours in the mills, has reduced hundreds of our fellow-townspeople to a state of misery and wretchedness that can scarcely be described'.

When it seemed that things couldn't get any worse for the people of Belfast, they did. The winter of 1846-47 was one of the most severe in living memory. Snow fell heavily and lay for weeks. Temperatures plunged to well below freezing point and stayed there. The poor who were doing their best to overcome the pangs of extreme hunger then had the constant cold to cope with as well.

Although the town's wealthier residents were not as drastically affected as the poor, and although trade continued to flourish in the main thoroughfares and the harbour seemed to be bustling with an increasing number of ships, the position of those beset by poverty and hunger was fast becoming desperate.

The conditions in which these people lived and into which the missionaries sought to bring some joy and comfort is reflected in a journal entry made by Mr. Shannon, an agent of the Town Mission, at that time.

'I was asked to go to see a poor family in Mary Street,' he wrote. 'I found them in an awful condition. Three were in the same bed unwell, two were at the day asylum almost as ill, two had lately risen, and were a little better, and one, a lodger, was sleeping on a little pallet in another corner, very low. There were only the two beds for the whole family and one of them was occupied entirely by the stranger. I was told it was fever they suffered from, but, after inquiry, I believe their sickness, of whatever kind, arises more from cold and hunger than anything else. These people from Ballyronan were forced to come to Belfast through lack of employment.'

Despite their best efforts, the many agencies which had been set up to deliver soup and bread to the starving were unable to cater for all those in immediate need. With the situation critical Queen Victoria declared that March 24, 1847 was to be observed as a day of prayer and fasting across the country. Her Proclamation met with a mixed response. The better off spent the day enjoying themselves, those who were not so fortunately fixed felt bitter at losing a day's pay, and for the destitute, fasting was no big deal. They were doing it every day anyway.

The Christians of the town, however, including those in many of the main churches and the town missionaries in their districts took it seriously. They knew that in such a time of famine their only hope lay in praying to the God who had directed Joseph through years of famine in Bible times. They opened their churches and meeting-places and invited all who wished to join them in beseeching God for His help.

William M 'Comb, the former secretary to the Mission, expressed the sentiments of the earnest God-fearing community in the town in a poem which he wrote, urging observance of the Queen's decree. He titled it, 'Call To Prayer.'

Heralds, as in days of Esther,
Make the Royal Message known,
Days of solemn prayer appointed,
God acknowledged from the throne.

Fathers, mothers, sisters, brothers,
Every family apart,
Bow before the throne of mercy,
Bend the knee and lift the heart.

Queen of England's proud dominions,
Princes, nobles of the land,
Pastors, people, ruled and rulers,
Bend the knee and lift the hand.

When Jehovah hath withholden
From the poor their daily bread,
When the famishing are dying,
Bend the knee, and bow the head.

Rich and poor obey the summons,
Loud the message comes to all,
When the Lord in wrath hath smitten,
Prostrate at His footstool fall.

In the hour of tribulation,
To the house of God repair;
Lay your gifts upon the altar,
Faith, and penitence, and prayer.

Yet another tragedy was to befall the town in that same month, March 1847. An emigrant ship from Liverpool was forced to seek refuge from bad weather in the port of Belfast. What nobody knew, though, when the 'Swatara' docked was that she had typhus on board. When the virus was carried ashore the fever swept through the weakened population with great speed.

Within months the disease had spread across the entire town. Dr. Malcolm, a local physician described it as, 'a plague of typhus, in comparison with which all previous epidemics were trivial and insignificant'.

The Hospitals were extended, temporary sheds' were erected, buildings used during the 1832 cholera epidemic were reopened and still the hastily appointed Board of Health couldn't cope. There just wasn't room for all those who were ill. Many were left to die in their filthy, ill-ventilated hovels. It was common to see helpless, hopeless people lying dying on the footpaths where they had fallen.

At the height of the epidemic in July fifty people were dying every day.

Disregarding the danger to themselves, and their families, the faithful missionaries of the Town Mission continued their quiet personal ministry at this time of crisis. They visited the homes of the sick in their district bringing as much aid as they could to those in need, and comfort to those who had lost loved ones. On many occasions they were able to alert the already grossly overstretched Board of Health to cases of which they were not aware up until that time.

The contribution of these humble servants of the Lord to the relief of many in the midst of suffering was acknowledged in an article in the *Belfast News-Letter.*

It reported that 'these faithful missionaries braved every danger, unmindful of every consideration, save the one great aim of mitigating the moral plague which they knew to be as widespread as the physical pestilence. Escaping the contagion which made such sweeping desolation all around, they were made the means of pouring the balm of hope and consolation into many a heart, which, in health and plenty, was closed against the admonition of the missionary, but which sorrow and suffering had at last subdued.'

The twentieth annual meeting of the Belfast Town Mission was held on October 18, 1847, almost at the end of a most difficult year for everyone. The respect which the Mission had come to command in the town was demonstrated in the fact that one thousand six hundred people packed into Dr. Henry Cooke's May Street Church for the occasion.

Many stirring reports were present but none more moving than those given by the two men who had been at the forefront of the Mission's battle against sin, sickness and starvation in the difficult years of forty-six and forty-seven.

Rev. William Johnston, who had been instrumental in helping to set up Soup Kitchens, highlighted one useful, but totally inadequate, effect of the work in a house he had visited.

. "When I entered the house," he told the hushed audience, "it was in vain that I looked for the smallest article of furniture. The hungry mother and six emaciated children were seated in the centre of the floor, with a basin, containing two quarts of soup, which had been received from the Soup Kitchen, placed before them. That was all they had to satisfy the cravings of hunger during the entire day."

In his report, Rev. Dr. Edgar began, 'Eighteen hundred and forty-seven is soon to close, and many a closing scene it has beheld. There ' have been last scenes of expiring prosperity and hopeless ruin. There have been last scenes of fading health and fatal sickness; last partings, last looks, and last farewells...'

He went on to tell how that through all the misery that they had encountered, they had also witnessed the hand of God at work. Tears had rolled down cheeks that had been dry from infancy. Hard hearts had been broken and become more receptive to the Gospel. Missionaries had been welcomed into homes that would otherwise have been closed to them.

In spite of all the hardships they had faced, and all the plague-ridden homes they had entered, motivated by the love God and the spread of the Gospel, all the missionaries had been preserved in health. This evoked a note of praise to God from Dr. Edgar as he concluded his report.

"Let it be, to those who know the loving kindness of the Lord," he urged, "a subject of special thanksgiving, that through pestilence and death, a gracious Providence has led our missionaries safe, and that amidst closing eyes, and sinking hearts, and heaving graves, they are all able to say, 'Hitherto hath the Lord helped us'".

6

A WONDERFUL WAVE OF DIVINE MERCY

The seeds of concern, sown in the minds of many of the poor people of Belfast by the ravages of the famine, continued to bear occasional fruit in the next decade. The Town missionaries kept on visiting homes stricken by poverty, disease and drunkenness, offering personal comfort and reading the scriptures. They also carried on their regular Sabbath Schools and evening services in their preaching stations, presenting the Gospel, and encouraging everyone to identify with a local church congregation.

These seeds of concern, which had been germinating in the hearts of the population of Ulster, and were watered by the prayers of a number of faithful and earnest Christians in Kells, County Antrim, yielded an abundant spiritual harvest across the province in 1859. This was a harvest in which the agents of the Belfast Town Mission, because of their intimate knowledge of the poorer districts of the town, were ideally equipped to assist.

On the first Sunday in June 1859, Rev. Robert Knox, minister of Linenhall Street Church, invited two converts from Connor, County Antrim, to address his congregation. The church was crowded. As the two young men read various scripture texts and spoke of the marvellous change that God had brought about in their lives, and in the lives of many others in their district, through His salvation, a woman fell down in her pew and cried out audibly for mercy. This was unusual, but not at that moment considered significant, for some claimed that the lady concerned had 'always been of weak mind'.

Two days later, on the following Tuesday evening, however, Rev. Hugh Hanna asked the same two young believers if they would like to tell of their experiences of the revival, which was sweeping across County Antrim, in his church in Berry Street.

Again the church was packed, and at this meeting a young man and a young woman cried out in spiritual anguish. Cynics could have attributed their singular convictions to hysteria also, but there could be no mistaking what happened after the meeting had been formally closed.

Nobody moved!

When it became evident that the congregation was reluctant to leave the building a spontaneous prayer meeting began. Within an hour two others had been brought under conviction of sin in such a way as made a profound impression on the audience. The church was filled with a tangible, almost terrifying, sense of the presence of God.

The '59 revival had come to Belfast.

The next evening, the Wednesday, was to be the mid-week prayer meeting in Berry Street Presbyterian Church. There was no minister present, but as the elders began to lead the large congregation in prayer many turned, in tears, to God for salvation.

Realising that God had begun to work in a mighty way in the town, Rev. Hanna and his elders determined to hold a meeting every night of the week for the foreseeable future so that seeking souls could find the Saviour. What had begun in Berry Street was followed immediately by similar visitations of the Spirit of God in salvation right across the town.

In churches where the ministers were leading figures in the Town Mission, for example Great George's Street, with Rev. Thomas Toye, Townsend Street, the church of Rev. William Johnston and Fisherwick Place, in the charge of Rev. Dr. Morgan, similar scenes were witnessed.

These and other Presbyterian Churches in common with some Church of Ireland, and some Methodist Churches arranged extra services to accommodate the constant stream of seeking souls.

The missionaries of the Town Mission were caught up in this movement of God from its very beginning in Belfast. As they conducted their own meetings in the month of June many who had been attending for months, possibly even years, came to know the Lord. Others, deeply distressed, were pointed to the Saviour in their own homes. Most of these missionaries had links with one of the larger Presbyterian Churches where the nightly meetings left many anxious souls waiting to be counselled, and new converts to be visited in their homes.

To them it was a thrill to be involved in this work. They had prayed for such a movement of the Spirit as this, but like Rhoda at the gate in the Bible, with Peter knocking to get in, could barely believe it. One missionary, gave as his reason for not attending some function which he deemed of lesser importance than the work which had overtaken he and his colleagues like a tidal wave, 'I am involved in the blessed necessity of a spiritual awakening.'

One of the most memorable days in the progress of the spiritual revival in Belfast was when one of the biggest crowds ever assembled in the metropolis of the north came together in a single location for a day of prayer. Despite the misgivings of some about the advisability of bringing so many people together in one place this special union day of prayer was arranged for Wednesday June 29 in the Botanic Gardens.

And what a gathering, and time of outpoured blessing, that proved to be!

Trains packed with hymn-singing people converged on the town's stations from many outlying areas. Men, women, and children walked in orderly fashion to the Gardens from all the different districts of the town.

Every gate was besieged by people pouring into the park. When the members of the platform party looked down, all they could see was a sweep of upturned faces, stretching off into the distance in all directions. The more able young men had done a Zacchaeus and climbed up into the branches of the trees, from where they could have a better view of proceedings while also leaving more precious space on the ground.

And still the people poured in through the gates!

When the scheduled time of commencement arrived more that thirty thousand people had congregated to praise God and pray for yet more blessing.

It soon became obvious, when Rev. John Johnston, Moderator of the General Assembly, began to address the vast audience, that those on the fringes of the crowd weren't going to be able to hear anything of the platform speeches or prayers. They overcame this in a very practical way by forming themselves into groups of between five hundred and a thousand people and setting up separate fervent prayer sessions. One observer was thrilled to record that 'in many parts of the gardens groups of boys and girls, many of them ragged, had evidently belonged to the outcast classes, prayed in language most affecting and impressive'. 'The outcast classes' were the people amongst whom the Town Mission had been established to work, and the results of years of faithful labour were beginning to be witnessed.

Although such a tremendous company had assembled, and although there were various groups praising God and praying aloud at a number of points across the entire expanse of the Botanic Gardens there was never any sense of chaos or confusion that day.

There were, though, many who cried to God for salvation, as the afternoon advanced. Others wept silently. Dozens came to know the Lord. And still the prayer and praise ascended, unabated.

When the crowd eventually dispersed as evening approached, and walked in orderly fashion, almost procession, back to their homes in different parts of the town, or to their train stations, many groups sang hymns of praise to God.

That evening hundreds, a good number of whom had been at the meeting of the multitude in the Gardens, flocked to the weekly united prayer meeting which had been started in the Music Hall (later to become Victoria Memorial Hall) in May Street. Others swarmed to the many churches where Gospel services were being conducted.

Rev. Thomas Toye related what happened in his own Church in Great George's Street the following evening. 'The people gathered in such numbers on June 30 that there was not accommodation for them; and there was one congregation in the church and two in the street. After the service in the church began there were piercing cries for mercy in every part of the house. There is a garden behind the church, into which there is an entrance from it, and several persons under conviction were removed thither, while others were taken into my own dwelling house,' he reported.

When the normal time for dismissal came nobody troubled to go home. Those who had been counselled in the garden of the church remained there until five o'clock in the morning, exhorting, praying and praising God. There were forty people saved that night in such a scene as Rev. Toye claimed had not 'been witnessed in Belfast before'.

Rev. William Johnston reported that every aspect of his congregation had been affected by this remarkable manifestation of the power of God. The careless had been convicted and converted, formalists who had been 'going through the motions' had found peace and joy in believing, backsliders had been restored, and 'the children of God' had been 'wondrously and blessedly revived'.

In such a time of spiritual awareness the missionaries of the Belfast Town Mission availed themselves of every opportunity to both contact the unsaved with the message of the Gospel or to encourage new Christians in their faith.

In Ewart's Row, a linen manufacturing area on the north side of town, a large number of the 'mill-girls' came to know Christ as their Saviour. This was a challenge to the Christians working amongst them. They rose to it admirably, though, with some workers linked to Berry Street Presbyterian Church arranging for Ewart's Row School to be opened for prayer, and also for classes in reading, writing and arithmetic three evenings per week. Christian friends, and Town missionaries joined in the good work and God richly blessed their efforts.

The new converts were so eager to learn to read, so that they could read the Bible for themselves, that they were no problem to teach. Within months some of them had learnt to read fairly acceptably, some had learnt to write 'a beautiful hand, and a few had 'advanced considerably in arithmetic'.

One such girl, who had come to know the Lord in Berry Street Church, and who had attended the prayer-meetings and classes in Ewart's Row School, reported, that 'the good done in every direction is incalculable. The Lord has done great things for us. The change witnessed in this locality is astonishing. The leisure hours were formerly devoted to boisterous amusements, in which profane swearing was practised to a fearful extent. Now the name of God is never heard, but with reverence, on any lips. Ewart's Row has been regenerated!'

Belfast was experiencing not only a spiritual, but also a social, renewal!

The revival was also marked by an increase in the numbers of children attending the Sabbath Schools run by the Town Mission and in the churches, and by the conversion of many of these young people. Dr. Morgan reported that in his church in Fisherwick Place the work was more marked in the Sabbath School than in the general congregation. Children who had once been inattentive began to show a genuine and respectful interest in the truth presented, and many of these young people yielded their lives to the Lord.

And so it went on through the summer and into the autumn of 1859.

Visiting evangelists Brownlow North and Rev. Grattan Guinness addressed large outdoor meetings with many people crying out for mercy and turning to Christ for salvation.

William M 'Comb, former secretary of the Mission was a witness of the sensational revelation of Sovereign grace that swept the province of Ulster and the town of Belfast in those days and recorded his observations in verse. With its message in the last verse for children it is possible that this poem was written to be read or recited in the Sabbath Schools.

THE REVIVAL OF 1859

Blow the trumpet, loud and long!
Sound the timbrel! Raise the song!
Through the nation flows salvation,
Blessing them of lowly station;

Zion's gates the poor ones throng:
There is knocking at the door,
Never, never, heard before.

Marvel not the poor are fed,
While the rich are lacking bread:
Golden treasures, earthly pleasures,
Are at best deceitful measures.
God has now a table spread;
Those who hunger are supplied;
Those who hunger not, denied.

Lo! The Holy Spirit's near,
Breathing pardon to the ear;
Souls releasing, sin decreasing,
Love to God and man increasing;
Scattering every doubt and fear:
Hearts and homes with peace abound,
Shedding happiness around.

Ne'er since Pentecostal hour
Fell a more refreshing shower;
Sleepers waking, sinners quaking,
Dry bones in the valley shaking;
Jesus, in His day of power,
Making bare His arm to win
Souls from Satan and from sin.

Now the waters reach in haste
From the ankles to the waist,
Rushing, rising, earth surprising;
Far too pure for analysing:
To a river now increased.
Sinner! Plunge, and reach the shore,
Washed and healed for evermore.

Children! Come, increase your joy;
Every gift and grace employ:
Upward doing! Still pursuing,

Pisgah's lofty summit viewing;
Nought can here your peace destroy.
Trust in Christ, believe and live:
HE alone can succour give.

At the Annual Meeting of the Town Mission held on November 9, 1859, Rev. Dr. Edgar summarised in his report the contribution of the work of the Mission to the breaking of 'that wonderful wave of Divine mercy' upon the town of Belfast.

"The Town Mission was never so honoured as during the past year," he told a capacity audience in Dr. Cooke's May Street Church. "In the spirit of profound gratitude to the Sovereign Author of all Grace, the Committee feel called on to bear testimony to the remarkable outpouring of the Holy Spirit on every one of the districts, and on the labours of all the missionaries. That wonderful wave of Divine mercy which has so enriched our Province, has visited this Mission in an especial manner. In the brevity that must be observed in the present report it is not possible to describe the nature and fruits of that visitation as exhibited among the poor of Belfast. While most of the congregations of the town have shared in the blessing, we believe it has fallen in greatest abundance on the class who come under the care of this Mission. For many years we have been sowing the good seed, breaking up the fallow ground, looking and praying for the harvest. That harvest has come at last, and in such a measure as we never ventured to hope for. The Spirit of the Lord has breathed upon the seed, and has given it life, and already there appears a glorious ingathering of precious souls. We do not thus speak merely because of increased attendance at Sabbath Schools and Prayer Meetings, or because of intense earnestness among the people, but from the testimony of Christian men competent to judge the manifestation of the fruits of the spirit. We thus speak because we believe that hundreds of immortal souls have been born again, and are now adorning the doctrine of God their Saviour."

All the faithful but often lonely, and occasionally even apparently fruitless work of the missionaries in 'sowing the good seed and breaking up the fallow ground' had been rewarded in a wonderful way.

An article in the Belfast News-Letter also acknowledged the input of the missionaries to the spiritual revival amongst the people of the town, almost a year later, on October 27, 1860. Reflecting on that period of 'quickening and refreshing grace', it stated, 'During the Revival of the past year the Belfast Town Mission was signally blessed. The number of persons drafted from it and by it into the churches may be reckoned by thousands. The people had been gathered during the many years previously into prayer meetings, and Bible Classes, and when the tide of living waters flowed through the town they were borne into the House of God, and are now among the most earnest and regular occupants of the pews there. The work of excavation and preliminary training was effected by the missionaries, so that when the quickening and refreshing grace was given as a plenteous shower, a rich harvest was gathered. There is still, however, a vast work to be accomplished."

It was thrilling to be caught up in such a dramatic demonstration of Divine grace but the blessings of the revival had presented the Committee and missionaries of the Town Mission with challenges they had never encountered before on such a scale.

New Christians had to be instructed in the faith, an unprecedented demand for Bibles had to be met, and new accommodation had to be either built or acquired to house those seeking to hear the Word of God.

And in addition to all of that, the population of the town was still rising rapidly.

By 1860 there were one hundred and twenty thousand people living within the boundaries of Belfast, and half of those never attended a place of worship. Many of them were living in poverty in the overcrowded courts and lanes of the town and despite the wonderful transformation in the lives of thousands who had come to Christ, there were thousands more who had still never heard the life-changing message of the Gospel.

It was true.

There was still a vast work to be accomplished.

7

LABOURING IN HOPE

Little did the poor people in the streets and lanes of Belfast, and the struggling flax spinners in the rural counties of Ulster know, but a Civil War which had broken out in America in 1861was to bring about considerable improvements in their job opportunities.

Northern ships blockaded the ports of the southern cotton growing states. This had the immediate effect of cutting off the supply of raw cotton to Britain. The busy mills of Lancashire were forced to cut down on production and a world shortage of cotton goods resulted.

Linen took its place.

Demand soared and the Belfast mill-owners responded with immediate enlargement.

The number of power looms in the town trebled in six years, from three thousand in 1862 to nearly nine thousand in 1868. Seven new weaving factories were opened and existing firms expanded their spinning and weaving operations.

With relatively cheap railway travel available and the prospect of employment in the rapidly developing linen industry a dream to chase, an endless stream of hopeful humanity continued to surge towards Belfast from all directions. Some of these immigrants were successful in finding work, but not all of them had the same success in securing a home of their own. New building couldn't keep pace with increased demand and it was not uncommon to find three, four or even five families sharing the one set of rooms.

This ever-upward trend in the population of Belfast, combined with a quickened spiritual awareness as a result of the '59 revival and the diligent work of the Town missionaries led to developments in the organisation of the Mission. By 1864 there were twenty Presbyterian churches in the town and four of them, and to a certain extent a fifth, had been erected through the instrumentality of the Town Mission.

In an attempt to reach farther out into the sprawling growth surrounding bulging Belfast, while continuing to advance the work in its existing locations, in the mid-1860's the Town Mission drew distinct geographical boundaries for each of its twelve districts. Each of these areas was to be served by an agent, or missionary, under the control of a superintendent. These full-time agents were, in turn, ably assisted by a battery of Christian volunteers from the church congregations. There were nearly two hundred of these, chiefly young, men and women who taught in the Mission's Sabbath Schools and helped on occasions with the district visitation.

At that time also, the Town Mission Committee restated, for its supporters, the five departments in which each Missionary laboured. The spread of spiritual work in which each man was engaged shows that these servants of the Lord and of the poor of Belfast were men who worked more for love than money. The journals that each man was expected to keep indicate that, despite setbacks and disappointments, God blessed their efforts on many occasions.

It was the responsibility of each missionary to arrange a meeting in the centre of his district on the Sabbath for the preaching of the Gospel. This was always held in the evening to avoid clashing with the morning service in the local churches, and for another altogether more practical reason. Men who had been 'out on the town' on a Saturday night were more likely to be sober by Sunday evening. Congregations, comprised mainly of the poor people of the town, weren't expected to dress up in their 'Sunday best' to attend Town Mission services. Many of them didn't have a 'best', and counted themselves blest, to have an 'only' outfit. A shawl pulled up over a woman's head was all that was expected by way of a head covering.

During the week the missionary conducted at least one prayer meeting in his district. In order to make this meeting available to as many of the people of the area as possible it was often scheduled for a different location each week in a three or four week cycle.

The weekly Bible Class was another meeting which the missionary was expected to lead with the young men in his area. The purpose of this gathering was to instruct the young in the principles of the Word of God and to see them 'built up in their most holy faith'.

Recognising the importance of presenting the Gospel to young and receptive hearts, each missionary was responsible for conducting at least one Sabbath School in his district. With an increasing emphasis being put on education, even of the poor, and with the opening of a number of day schools across the town, many children were happy to attend Sabbath School as well, and many of these were large. In every district there were at least two Sabbath Schools, often morning and afternoon in the same place. In some there were as many as four, using a variety of venues and starting times to allow the maximum number of children possible to be reached.

The Town Mission used neutral, non-denominational buildings in which to conduct the majority of the meetings in their districts. Schools and mills were the most frequently used locations. The Sabbath Schools in Welsh Street School, Brown Square School and Lagan Village School were the biggest in the town, each of them attracting well over one hundred children every Sunday.

The missionaries considered it a privilege to be able to tell these children, many of whom knew little of earthly comfort, of the love of God and the joy that was to be found in trusting Jesus. The Sabbath School was the highlight of the day for many children who were destined to spend the remainder of the day playing in the streets and lanes where they lived.

An excerpt from an agent's journal of the time expressed adequately the value that was placed both on the message taught to the children and the dedication of the teachers involved.

'Sabbath 30. With respect to the Sabbath school, I cannot report too favourably. The numbers are increased far beyond our greatest expectations. Last Sabbath there were present 136. The conduct of the children is remarkably good, when the class to which the majority of them belong is taken into consideration. The diligence and faithfulness of the teachers cannot be too highly commended. They are workmen who need not to be ashamed, their only desire being to advance the interest of the Messiah's kingdom in the success of the school, and in the salvation of souls. They are labouring in hope and praying for a blessing.'

Probably the most important part of the missionary's work and the one which occupied the greatest proportion of his time was house visitation. He spent at least four hours every day, Monday to Friday, visiting in the district. This systematic programme of calling from door to door, up and down street after street, was the key that opened the door to all the other branches of the mission. Without it neither the Sabbath School, the prayer meeting, the Bible Class nor the Sunday evening service could be carried on effectively.

When he called at any home the agent of the Town Mission read a portion of the scriptures and prayed with the occupants, if permitted. He also invited any children he met to attend the Sabbath School and everyone else in the home to become associated with the local church. Bibles and tracts were left in homes where the agent considered that there was both an ability to read, and sufficient interest to merit it.

These house calls brought the missionaries into daily contact with people who had no interest in spiritual matters and others who were physically incapable of attending any place of worship. It also, from time to time, afforded them unusual encouragements and evidences of the power of God in the Gospel through their ministry as two successive entries in the journal of one missionary would indicate.

'Friday, September 15, 1865. Today I visited a man dying of cancer in the tongue. He had been in Frederick

Street Hospital and was turned out to die, as being incurable. When I went in he said, "Oh sir, I know you. I heard you preaching in the open air last summer, and I remember what you said yet. It was, 'The words I have spoken unto you under this gable, if you despise them, will rise up as a swift witness to condemn you'"

" I never forgot those words," the dying man went on to articulate, with some difficulty.

His wife, who was sitting nearby, explained to me what he was saying, for I could not catch his words, owing to his indistinct articulation. She told me that she had often heard him repeat those words.

Then I asked him did he know Jesus and could he trust his soul in Christ's hands.

"Oh yes, I can. I am happy. I have given up all for Christ. Oh bless His name!" came the reply.

He appeared to be quite exhausted by the effort he made to speak, and I left, praising God in my heart for a soul snatched as a brand from the burning. He only heard the closing sentences of my discourse, and this one word, as mentioned above, was as the arrow of the Lord.

This incident shows that open-air services may be greatly blessed of God to the awakening of souls. I had almost forgotten all those services I held last year, but God had not forgotten the seed sown.'

Five days later he wrote,

'Wednesday, September 20. I found today that the poor man ill of cancer of the tongue had died a day or two ago. His deathbed was a triumph of saving grace. He passed away expressing his delight at the prospect of seeing the Saviour who washed him from his sins in His own precious blood. He also expected his family to follow him to the land of glory. His wife appeared resigned to the will of God, her Heavenly Father.'

This is but one example of many. When multiplied by twelve districts across Belfast and then by fifty-two for every week of the year it represents something of what was achieved for the advancement of the kingdom of Jesus Christ by the faithful agents of the Mission and their dedicated helpers. Their sole object was the salvation of souls and the only instruments they employed were the truth of God in the preaching of the Gospel and the teaching of the Word of God. They told the poor and wayward of the town of the infinite love of God and the death of His son Jesus Christ for their sin.

This alone, they knew, was what could bring peace, joy and holiness to the hearts and homes of the people.

So they would, with the eighteen highly commended teachers in the 4.30 p.m. Sabbath School in Welsh Street Schoolroom, continue 'labouring in hope and praying for a blessing.'

8

DEWDROPS FROM HEAVEN

In 1869, Dr. Henry Cooke and Dr. John Edgar, two men who had been influential in the organisation and operation of the Belfast Town Mission passed away to be with the Lord whom they had served so faithfully all their lives. Dr. Cooke, who had been minister of May Street Presbyterian Church, and also Vice-President of the Mission, had been a fearless exponent of the evangelical Christian cause in ecclesiastical and political circles. Dr. Edgar of Alfred Place Church had been a highly respected figure in the town. He was an honorary secretary of the Mission and as such had been one of its most eloquent supporters for many years. He was noted for his practical philanthropy and his powerful advocacy of Temperance in a town where one of the biggest problems the mission agents encountered in the homes they visited was drunkenness.

At the annual meeting of the Mission in November of that year, deep regret was expressed at their passing, and high tribute paid to the spiritual and eternal worth of their lives and labours, by all the speakers present.

However, as would have been their wish, the ongoing work of the mission had to be reviewed, with progress noted and changes considered where necessary.

On looking back, an encouraging aspect of the previous year was the opening of two new Presbyterian Churches in the town, one in Cromac Street and the other in Academy Street. In each of these cases a town Missionary had made contact with a large number of people in the area, and when these groups had approached the General Assembly they were granted permission to organise as separate and distinct congregations. Thus the establishment of these two churches could be related directly to the unremitting service of the agents.

While this expansion was gratifying and the leaders of the Mission were constantly urging everyone to praise God for His blessings yet they had come to recognise that they were not achieving one of their basic goals to its utmost extent. This was the aim of bringing 'the lapsed masses', the townspeople who were Presbyterian in name only, into active contact with existing churches. Many of these had been regular in their attendance at a place of worship in rural areas but on arriving in Belfast in search of work in the mills or at the harbour, hadn't been sufficiently interested to seek out a new church.

In an attempt to address that situation it was decided that the agents should be more closely affiliated to individual churches, as this would enable them to bring the people of the district along with them to a local focus of spiritual activity. It was proposed to assign each church a territorial district with the services of a missionary to be offered on the condition that the congregation provided half of his salary. Although liasing closely with the church minister about the immediate needs of the designated district, the missionary thus employed was to remain ultimately responsible to the committee of the Belfast Town Mission.

These proposals seemed to appeal to some for during the following year four churches, Townsend Street, First Ballymacarrat, Duncairn and Ekenhead agreed to pay for the upkeep of a Town missionary working in their church district. In the following year, 1871, two others, Clifton Street and Rosemary Street, recognising the potential benefits of having a missionary affiliated to their congregation, and possibly seeing positive results from the original four to adopt the scheme, followed suit.

The reallocation of districts to correspond with church locations resulted in the still rapidly expanding town being divided into twenty-four districts, but in 1871 there were still only fourteen missionaries serving them all.

The committee of the Mission would have dearly loved to see an agent employed in spreading the good news of the Gospel in every possible district but the finances to maintain such an ideal level of cover were not available. It was back to the perennial problem of money. The work of the Mission had grown remarkably and seen much accomplished for God since its establishment more than forty years before, but it had been constantly hampered by financial constraints.

An unusual, and heart-warming meeting in connection with the Town Mission was held in Fisherwick Place Schoolroom on Tuesday evening, March 25, 1873.

It had been the tradition of the Mission over many years to hold occasional social gatherings in connection with the Sabbath Schools and Bible Classes but on that date all the Sabbath School teachers from across the town had an evening especially to themselves.

The Committee of the Mission believed that the time had come to recognise the consistent work of these selfless servants of the poor and working classes, and more than two hundred of them responded to the personal invitations they had received.

Rev. William Johnston, who had become by then Moderator of the General Assembly, presided and extended a most hearty welcome to all.

When these teachers who had travelled from all parts of the town had spent a happy time sharing their experiences Rev. Dr. Knox announced that Mr. Charles Finlay had a gift for each teacher in recognition of his or her services and to help with further preparation. The thirteen missionaries present were then delighted to see the faithful teachers from their districts presented with a copy of either 'Patterson on the Shorter Catechism' or 'The Companion to The Bible'.

Later that same year Rev. Dr. James Morgan, one of the founder members of the Mission, and the man whose spiritual insight had brought William Cochrane, its first agent to Belfast, died.

Like some of the others who had passed on in the previous decade, Dr. Morgan's loss was keenly felt by those responsible for coordinating the work of the Belfast Town Mission. For more than forty years he had contributed much of his time, money and intense sympathy to the work and his godly wisdom combined with a genuine concern for the poor and underprivileged of the town, meant that his counsel was often sought, and appreciated.

Concluding his address at the funeral service in Rosemary Street Church on December 23, 1873, the Moderator exhorted those present to endeavour to follow in his footsteps in the service of the Lord.

"It now rests with others to carry on the great work originated and so fondly cherished by him," he proclaimed. "Let all those amongst us who have a compassion for the poor and those who are ready to perish, strive together to make this Town Mission one of the most noble and enduring monuments to his memory."

Those words would later seem almost prophetic for an opportunity was soon to arise for the eager agents of the Mission 'to carry on the great work originated and so fondly cherished' by Dr. Morgan in a most spiritually-rewarding way.

Exciting snippets of news of a spiritual revival in Edinburgh, something after the nature of what had happened fourteen of fifteen years before in Ulster, began to reach the Christian leaders in the town. An American evangelist called Dwight Moody and his associate Ira Sankey were being used of God to spearhead 'a religious awakening such as has not been seen since the days of Whitefield.'

Many of the leading evangelical ministers had lived through the blessed days of the '59 Revival, and longing to experience a further outpouring of the power of God they began to enquire, 'Shall we see no droppings of this heavenly dew in Belfast?'

During a week of prayer in January 1874, Presbyterian congregations were encouraged to 'pray for a portion of the same blessing which is so plentifully being given at Edinburgh'.

A few months later, a conference of ministers extended an invitation to Mr. Moody to come and conduct some meetings in Belfast, at his convenience. It was Rev. William Johnston, Moderator of the General Assembly, minister of Townsend Street Church, and life long supporter of the Town Mission who proposed that Moody and Sankey should be asked to visit the town, and this was seconded by Rev. Charles Seaver, of St. John's, Laganbank. Mr. Moody, impressed by the spirit of unity which appeared to exist amongst the evangelical churches in Belfast, accepted the invitation and it was to a number of praying, prepared and expectant churches that the well-known duo arrived in the early autumn of 1874.

During their first day of mission in Belfast on Sunday, September 6, Moody and Sankey held three services. The first of these was an early morning gathering for church workers in Donegall Square Methodist Church, the second was at 11.30 a.m. in Fisherwick Place church, and the evening service was held in the biggest church available in the town at the time, St. Enoch's.

There was an air of anticipation about the town, and all these services on that first day were crowded to the doors. The congregation that thronged into St. Enoch's was, according to one who had been present, 'one of the largest ever witnessed in Belfast'.

This trend continued.

The weeknight services were held in Rosemary Street Presbyterian Church but so many people came that other ministers had to hold overflow meetings in adjoining halls.

The interest grew.

On the second Sunday the early morning meeting for Christian workers was packed out well before the scheduled starting time. That afternoon an open-air meeting was held on open ground opposite Agnes Street Presbyterian Church and over twenty thousand people turned up.

Dewdrops from heaven had begun to descend on Belfast for a second time. Hundreds of people were counselled in the enquiry rooms which had become features of the American evangelists' campaigns, and many turned to Christ for salvation.

Another aspect of this Moody mission, and one in which the agents of the Town Mission had every opportunity to become involved, was the special gatherings targeted towards specific groups. There were meetings for 'females' on certain afternoons in Fisherwick Place Church, evening meetings for men in Rosemary Street and Linenhall Street, and Mr. Sankey himself led special children's meetings in May Street Presbyterian Church.

Many of the ministers and Christian leaders of the town had been present at the famous prayer meeting in Botanic Gardens during the earlier revival and so it was arranged that the final gathering of the Moody and Sankey campaign should be a massive evangelistic rally at the same venue.

This was held on the afternoon of Thursday, October 8, to allow anyone who wished to travel in on the specially chartered excursion trains to attend. The thirty-thousand crowd which flocked into Botanic Gardens through all its gates was in many ways reminiscent of what had happened more than fifteen years before. Only this time the meeting had been convened primarily for preaching and as Dwight L. Moody's voice boomed out over the vast crowd it could be 'heard distinctly at the farthest part of the meeting.' That same huge audience also listened with awe and respect as Mr. Sankey sang a selection of his hymns to them, and at the end of the service many were spoken to by specially chosen counsellors and gave their lives to Christ.

Although the town missionaries were thrilled to be caught up in another visitation of the Lord in Belfast their most important work was done in the aftermath of the mission. Moody and Sankey left the town on 'a spiritual high'.

Many souls had been saved, but there were many more who remained concerned about their condition and position before God. It was the privilege of the agents of the Mission to contact such people and lead them to faith. Then, throughout the winter that followed, special Gospel services were arranged across the town, and three of these concentrated evangelistic efforts were held in 'stations' run by the Mission in Brown Square School, Hemsworth Street School and the York Street Mill.

The Annual report of the Mission presented at the end of 1875 referred to the positive effect of the 'intense religious fervour' which had been 'awakened in the autumn of last year'.

'There is still a widespread thirsting for the Word of life,' was the stated conclusion of the joint secretaries, 'an unabated desire to hear the Gospel and a cordial welcome for the Missionary in the homes of the people. To meet this desire, some of the Missionaries have held Special Evangelistic Services every evening of the week, and sometimes for a period extending over several weeks. The testimony of the Missionaries is uniform to the fact that the influence of the awakening has been very precious and abiding among many of the poor, both old and young. Stolid indifference has given place to anxiety and earnestness, and while much fruit has been gathered, many are still eagerly 'enquiring the way to Zion'. Is it not a high privilege to work when the Master is saying, 'Behold I have set before you and open door, and no man can shut it'?

The Missionaries did appreciate the privilege to work for the Master on those terms and through the example of Moody and Sankey they had added a new weapon to their armoury in the battle against sin and every sort of social evil.

It was the special evangelistic campaign.

9

THE LOOK THAT PIERCED
A HEART

The increased spirit of anxiety and earnestness that pervaded all the meetings across the town at that time resulted in a bountiful harvest for God in many areas.

William Maxwell who was the missionary in charge of Durham Street district records that a number of conversions in which he was directly involved, took place during that Moody and Sankey mission.

One evening when he was acting as a counsellor in an enquiry room following a packed meeting in Fisherwick Place Church William sat down beside a woman who was weeping bitterly.

When he began to speak to her he discovered that the lady was a widow who longed to know the peace and joy of salvation in her soul. He read the scriptures to her and told her of the love of God, explaining how that His son, Jesus, had died on the cross to take away her sin and make her His child if she trusted in Him.

After some time the woman decided to leave, convinced that her case was hopeless, yet still in evident distress and still without the satisfaction of salvation.

Neither counsellor nor counselled spent a very restful night. The woman was in anguish of mind and soul and William Maxwell spent much of the night in prayer for her and for guidance from God for himself in dealing with the situation.

Leaving it to the early afternoon to allow her to attend to her housework in the morning, the town missionary called next day at the address she had given him. On being invited into her simple home the lady asked him to excuse the untidiness of the room for she had been unable to attend to her domestic duties, being so burdened about her soul.

They sat down together and William opened his Bible and began where he had left off the night before, reading different verses to her in an attempt to explain the way of salvation.

Then when he read Hebrews chapter nine and verse twenty-six the truth of the Gospel dawned upon her. On hearing the words, '...but now once in the end of the world hath he appeared to put away sin by the sacrifice of himself,' she realized that the sin that had been so perplexing her had been put away by Christ's death on the cross and on accepting that found peace in her soul.

William was then delighted to become a virtual spectator as the woman poured out her grateful heart in spontaneous praise to God for the joy that had come to her through trusting in Christ. He made a number of visits to her following that red-letter day in her life and found the lady progressing steadily in her Christian faith.

The case of John, who for many years had showed no interest whatsoever in anything but swearing and spending most of his wages on drink, was somewhat different.

John had been persuaded to attend a cottage meeting in the court where he lived but went without showing much concern. Then one evening in October 1874, as he was just going in through the door of a local public house he saw the young man who normally preached at the cottage meeting, passing.

Their eyes met.

Not a word was spoken but the earnest gaze of the regular speaker seemed to pierce right into the innermost being of the regular drinker, stopping him in his tracks.

He hadn't been long in the pub that evening until a great sense of unhappiness came over John. Spending the whole evening in the bar and most of his money on booze no longer appealed to him. He had to leave, no doubt much to the surprise of his normal drinking companions.

For days he struggled with this restlessness of spirit which had overtaken him. He gave up drinking but could still find no peace. Often during the working day he was compelled to shut himself away and pray to God for relief from this misery of soul, but nothing happened.

One morning at breakfast time he gathered his wife and family around him and told them that he had determined to lead a new life. They were pleased to hear of this resolve for if it worked it would make life so much more pleasant for them, but the resolve in itself didn't bring John the rest that he craved.

Someone told William Maxwell about him and he went to visit John at home. As they talked together about pardon for sin and peace with God he wept and said repeatedly, "Oh I wish I could get it! That's what I want! I wish I could get it!"

Having spoken to John for quite a while William left, telling him that he would be praying that God would help him to understand and accept the wonderful salvation that He had provided for the world, and that meant for him too.

Before leaving John's home William had invited the man who had become overwhelmed with spiritual turmoil to come along to the Sabbath service in his 'station' in Hutchinson Street School and on the following Sunday he turned up. After the service William Maxwell spoke to John again and he accepted Christ as his Saviour.

The long struggle for peace was over and John was overjoyed to find satisfaction in his soul and in his life. His conversion not only brought him personal peace but it also made a tremendous difference to the home situation. Now his wife was assured of a full pay packet coming home and the children had regular food to eat and decent clothes to wear.

The challenge of nurturing this new Christian in his faith was made increasingly difficult for the missionary, and all those who took a personal interest in John and his family, by the fact that they were every one illiterate. There was no point in giving them Bibles, as the missionaries often did with recent converts, because not a single one of them, neither John, his wife, nor any of his family could read!

Spiritual follow-up in this case would have to be taken slowly and simply, and would of necessity be accompanied by much earnest prayer and tender care. Satan would not give up one of his slaves without a struggle. William Maxwell was painfully aware of this. As an ardent agent of the Mission he had lived through those thrilling days of the Moody and Sankey Mission and its exciting spiritual repercussions, then the gradual lowering in religious fervour towards the end of the following year.

In December 1875 he recorded in his journal what could have been the personal testimony of many of the Town Missionaries in their different districts at that time.

'Looking back on the year just closed there is much in connection with the district, Durham Street, both to cheer and to discourage,' he wrote. 'The happy results of the Revival are still to be seen in many cases, in which those who professed conversion are adorning the doctrine of God their Saviour, while others, who seemed to start on the heavenly road, have gone back to the world and are worse than ever. Strong drink has proved a snare to several who appeared to have escaped the pollutions of the world through the knowledge of Jesus Christ'.

It is impossible to tell into which of William's clearly defined categories John fell.

We can only trust it was the former. Those who were continuing 'to adorn the doctrine of God their Saviour'.

10

THE STRUCTURE AT STRANMILLIS

The mushrooming linen mills in Belfast had employed mostly women but when Edward Harland and Gustav Wolff went into partnership in 1861 they continued to expand an industry which had already begun at the harbour, and which employed mainly men.

It was shipbuilding.

The growth of shipbuilding and other subsidiary engineering establishments led to a spectacular development in housing in Belfast in the late nineteenth century. Men working in the heavy engineering industries earned around three times the average wage of mill workers, whether male or female. This meant that the families who still continued to flood into the town from the country in search of work could afford the reasonable rents of the newly-erected kitchen and parlour houses which were being built at amazing speed into little streets radiating off virtually every road out of the town.

While these houses were being built by the thousand for the working classes, the development of the Belfast Street Tramways Company, with its fleet of double-decker tramcars and its hundreds of horses to pull them along shiny new metal tracks, brought with it another change in the housing pattern. The better off citizens began to build their own houses farther out of town on the routes served by the horse drawn trams. A host of houses clustered around the termini on the Malone Road, the Antrim Road and the Holywood Road, to name but three, meant that further housing began to become available in the town centre.

The face of Belfast and its pace of life were changing fast.

Belfast Town Mission struggled to cope with the challenges this presented. Despite the apparent economic boom, the poor would be with them always, and drunkenness was still a problem in many of the homes they visited. And much as they would have liked to place an agent in every new district their financial position hindered them from expanding their operations in any way proportionate to the phenomenal growth of the town.

Unfortunately, however, social and economic growth in the town could not provide its population with either political stability of permanent personal peace.

Arising out of the unrest generated by Mr. Gladstone's first Home Rule Bill in 1886 serious rioting broke out across the town that summer, greatly hampering the work of the Mission in its endeavours to reach out to the poor. Many of the people with whom the missionaries were in regular contact became caught up in the disturbances.

For four months, from early June until September, Belfast was in a constant state of turmoil. Rival factions confronted each other, and in many instances the police, almost every night.

The riots of 1886 in Belfast were the worst the town had experienced in the whole of the nineteenth century. By the time torrential rain fell for three days in September causing flooding and 'taking the heart out of all the fighting', according to one hardened combatant, fifty people had lost their lives, more than three hundred policemen and countless numbers of civilians had been injured, and the damage to property was incalculable.

That the bitter battles between the various groupings in the town deeply concerned and challenged the leaders of the Town Mission is evident from the annual report of that year, presented by Rev. James Maconaghie, an honorary secretary. Referring to the effects of crime and lawlessness in any town or society, he stated:

'The riots in our town during the past summer have painfully illustrated this fact. Lives and property were recklessly sacrificed, and deeds perpetrated and gloried in, of which we may feel heartily ashamed. Magistrates and clergymen who were present testify that the conduct of the crowd was that of infuriated demons, rather than that of a Christian town. Whilst deploring such an ebullition of angry and lawless feeling, with the fearful results that followed, may we not hope that the churches, taught by the lessons of the past, will interest themselves more heartily in the godless around them.

The recent events but show what a terrible reckoning must come where the masses are unreached by the elevating influences of the Gospel. And are we, as Christians, not guilty, in the sight of God and our fellowmen, with regard to such?

What sacrifices have we made, what efforts put forth, to raise them to a higher level? Have we earnestly sought their conversion, as we have done that of the Jew or the heathen? We dare not say that the souls of sinners are less precious because they live at our door.

We have not lost faith in the power of the Gospel. Surely then it is our bounden duty and privilege to reach such with the Word of Life, and pray God's Spirit to make it effective to their conversion.'

Rev. Maconaghie went on to outline the role of the Mission in attempting to address the challenges which the state of lawlessness in the town presented:

'Now this is just what our Town Mission, for more than forty years, has been striving to accomplish,' he said. 'Its Agents, by house-to-house visitation, tract distribution, services in halls, cottage meetings, Bibles classes and special evangelistic services, endeavour to bring souls to Christ and His Church. If the results have not been all that we could wish, the fault lies rather in the fewness of our Agents than in our organization or its working. What are some sixteen Missionaries to the thousands of spiritually-destitute they are supposed to

reach? And yet that God has highly honoured their work
is evident from their reports.'

After giving some facts and figures the secretary quoted from a
few of the missionaries reports to which he referred. One of these is
most interesting for it demonstrated that the agents of the Mission
were aware of the opportunities that existed for the spread of the
Gospel in a flourishing seaport.

The missionary related how that when visiting the ships in the
harbour he met a sailor who had not been to a place of worship for
several years. Having established a friendly relationship with him
the missionary invited the sailor to accompany him to the evening
service in a church. He came and began to attend church regularly
when in port.

Many months elapsed before the missionary saw his friend again
but when he did the sailor had encouraging news for him.

"I see it now," he said. "I am a changed man."

The missionary was willing to accept that what he had seen was
the transforming truth of salvation though Jesus Christ, for his whole
appearance and demeanour corroborated his testimony.

He was, indeed, 'a changed man'.

In 1889 the Mission Committee appointed Mr. William Maxwell,
who had been an active agent for fifteen years, to the position of
Financial Secretary. It was felt that the only way in which the
Christian public could be made aware of the valuable work of the
Mission and its crippling financial constraints was to appoint
someone with thorough practical knowledge of all its operations to
a full time position.

Counting himself privileged to promote a work so dear to his
heart William Maxwell assumed his responsibilities with diligence.
In his first year in office donations to the Mission increased by over
one hundred pounds and a fresh impetus was given to all its activities.
Ministers, missionaries and interested members of the public were
pleased to know that there was now a full-time man with an office in
May Street, to whom they could come for advice or information.

Although the first Home Rule Bill had been defeated the issue
came into prominence again in 1892 when Mr. Gladstone promised

that if he were re-elected in the General Election in August he would introduce a Bill to give Ireland a Parliament of her own. The Unionist community in Belfast, having been somewhat discredited by the riots of six years before, decided to present a huge, but peaceful and orderly protest, to such a move.

To do this they invited twelve thousand delegates from all over Ulster to demonstrate their opposition by assembling for a mass rally in the Botanic Gardens on Friday 17 June 1892. This massive all-seated gathering was accommodated in a specially designed convention hall erected within the space of three weeks on the Plains at Stranmillis.

A reporter for the Northern Whig described the purpose-built structure:

> 'The building covers one acre, the glass in the roof being about one third of an acre in extent. It is the largest which has ever been constructed in Great Britain or Ireland for political purposes, being 224 feet in the front and running back for about 150 feet.'

When the speeches were over and the delegates had all returned home on their special trains to destinations as far apart as Ballymena and Ballyroney, the huge temporary edifice remained silent and empty on its site beside the Lagan. The men who had put it up in three weeks were not in any hurry to take it down.

Recognising the potential of such a building for the declaration of the Gospel, a number of the evangelical Churches in the town formed a Campaign Committee. Then upon securing the use of the temporary convention hall they invited Mr. D.L Moody to return to the town in the autumn.

Large crowds converged on the hall for what was to be D.L. Moody's last visit to Ireland. Mr. J.H. Burke was his song-leader on that occasion and as the American evangelist could only stay for two weeks Rev. John Mc Neill, a Scottish evangelist continued the meetings for a further two-week period.

Although many of the town missionaries were active in their support of the Moody and Mc Neill meetings in the giant glass-roofed structure at Stranmillis, and though many souls came to know Christ as Saviour at that time, the real benefit to the Mission was, as had been the case nearly twenty years before, in the days that followed.

During that year the Mission committee had appointed two full time evangelists to assist the missionaries in their districts and as they held special meetings in various parts of Belfast in the winter following the autumn mission, they experienced much blessing.

In their annual report for 1892 the leaders of the Town Mission stated:

> 'During the past year, though the Moody-Mc Neill Mission only touched the fringe of the class among whom our agents work, the wave of Divine awakening which swept over our city reached some of our centres. Crowded meetings, anxious enquirers waiting to be spoken to, professed conversions and reformed drunkards all told that the power of the Lord was present to bless. At some of these meetings men long hardened through drink and sin have not only made a new start in life, but are also the Missionary's most zealous helpers.'

The work was progressing, and in the next year, 1893, the Committee and Agents of the Mission would have much to reflect upon, and much for which they would wish to praise God, for the Re-organised Town Mission would by then have been reaching out to the poor of Belfast for fifty years.

11

THE YEAR OF JUBILEE

On November 7, 1888, Queen Victoria issued a charter conferring 'the rank, privileges and immunities incident to a city upon Belfast'. This presented the local council, which was then meeting in the Town Hall in Victoria Street, with a dilemma. They had just been elevated to the rank of a City Council, and a City Council needed a City Hall.

They went on work on this problem, and when they had acquired the site of the White Linen Hall in Donegall Square they had plans drawn up and built an ornate and appropriate City Hall.

The promotion to city status also meant that the Belfast Town Mission was stretching out with the light and love of the Gospel into the spiritual darkness of the streets and lanes of a city.

For years, though, they made no change.

There were more immediate issues to be confronted.

What did a name or title matter when there were hundreds of little children in Belfast who had never heard the name of Jesus? Thousands of people all over the new city were dying without ever having had any contact with Christ or a church.

There was much to be done with families still continuing to arrive in the city from the country on a daily basis. The missionaries were kept constantly busy. There were new streets to be visited, an increasing number of meetings to be conducted and former contacts to be maintained and nourished until they ripened eventually into a harvest for God.

Mr. William Maxwell was a former missionary himself, and someone who appreciated at first hand the delights and disappointments of the calling. As such he must have considered it part of his new role as permanent financial secretary to the Mission to inform the comfortable church-going public of the valuable but often unseen and unsung service of these faithful men of God.

In the early 1890's he followed in the footsteps of the first honorary secretary of the Mission, William McComb, by expressing his sentiments in verse. His poem entitled 'The City Missionary' was first read at an annual meting and having been much appreciated was later published to help draw attention to the diverse nature of the missionary's mission for his Master.

It is most enlightening and worth quoting…

Aside from busy highways, far behind
The fashionable square,
In dingy court or alley you may find
The objects of His care.

Where ebbing life on yonder attic floor
Helpless and anguished lies,
He sheds a light around the open door
To life that never dies.

Now hastening thence some fainting heart to cheer,
Whose path is rough and steep:
Anon he follows some lone pauper's bier
To where the nameless sleep.

The little children gratefully return
The good man's smile so kind,
As though they did instinctively discern
His Master's love behind.

In yonder meeting place, with earnest speech
He plies the sons of toil;
Intent and prayerful that the truth may reach
Some stony hearts the while.

He yearns to help the fallen rise again,
The rescued ones to place
'Mid goodly fellowship of saintly men,
And see them grow in grace.

Thus 'neath the surface of our city life,
Oft in its depths obscure,
This Christian diver toils, where wrecks are rife,
His trophies to secure.

Nor shall the King his servant's name forget
(Unknown to earth's renown),
In that great day when rescued souls are set
 As jewels in His crown.

One of those rescued souls, one of those jewels, will most certainly be the young woman who was contacted by John Beattie, one of the missionaries.

While visiting in his district near the city centre one day John spoke to an attractive young woman, whom we shall call Mary, who, he was to discover, was living a life of sin on the streets. In course of conversation he invited her to a meeting in one of the local churches but she declined, asking quite pointedly, "What have people like me got to do with you and your churches?"

The missionary continued to press his invitation, which the woman persisted in refusing.

As he was turning to leave her, Mary said, completely unexpectedly, "Are you not Mr. Beattie?"

Trying to disguise his surprise, the missionary replied, "Yes, I am. But how do you know me?"

"I belonged to your Congregational Sabbath School years ago," came the confession. "When I started work, though, I began to drink and one thing led to another. I have no desire at all to go back to your church meetings."

John Beattie was downhearted, as he had no other option but to leave Mary standing stubborn in the street, but vowed to request prayer for her.

Three months later two other strange young women appeared at John's house one evening with a request. They asked him if he would call to someone who was dying in the Workhouse Hospital. This person, a woman, kept asking for him, it seemed.

The missionary set off immediately and found that the person requesting the visit was none other than Mary whom he had met in the street in the slums.

What a change there was in that young lady! The body that had once been so attractive was now gaunt and grey, held in the grip of a terminal illness. The spirit that had once been both carefree and careless had now been overcome with conviction of sin.

"Oh Mr. Beattie I am glad to see you!" the dying woman burst out when the missionary arrived at her bedside. "I need to know peace in my soul!"

John Beattie was delighted to be afforded the opportunity to open his Bible and point her to the Son of God who died on the cross to atone for the sin of the world, and after some time Mary accepted Christ as her Saviour.

From that moment she was a transformed person and for the remaining few months of her life she testified to the others in the hospital of the peace she had found through trusting in Jesus. All those who knew Mary said that her last days were full of the brightest joy and thanksgiving.

What a trophy to secure!

The Jubilee Meeting of the Belfast Town Mission, which was more a social than a formal event, was held on Friday, February 9, 1894.

When presenting his report, Rev. James Maconaghie, honorary secretary, reminded the large audience that on that occasion they were reviewing the work of not only one, but of fifty years.

'We are justly proud of the rapid strides our town

has made over the last half century' he began. 'Our costly and imposing warehouses and shops, our handsome public buildings, our large and various manufactories, our fine streets and beautiful villas, and our proverbial business energy excite the admiration of those visiting our city. Yet all these are largely the growth of the last fifty years. Would that our religious history during this period were as bright and encouraging. True, churches and schools have greatly increased, our Ministers are as active and efficient as their predecessors were, and our church organisations have also multiplied...'

Having begun with the positive aspects of their town turned city, the speaker went on to present the other side of the coin.

'Yet the painful cry still falls on our ears that an increasing proportion of our population are drifting away from both the Churches and the Christ. They who tell us this are not alarmists. Our missionaries testify that there are streets in which at the most not one in every ten ever enters a church or hall to hear the good news of salvation...'

In spite of the task still facing them, the Mission had made significant progress over those fifty years.

In 1843, when the mission had been re-organised, there were five agents, or missionaries, employed. In 1893 there were eighteen.

In 1893 many more homes had been visited, many more meetings and Sabbath Schools had been held, and many more families had been encouraged to join churches, than in 1843.

However, the population of Belfast had increased from just over 70, 000 in 1843 to around 300,000 in 1893 and the extension of the mission was still struggling valiantly to keep up with the pace of expansion in the town in which they served their Lord.

Having given a list of facts and figures the secretary went on to say that spiritual, not numerical, results were the most important element of their work but they were also totally impossible to tabulate. The high point of the previous year, and indeed of every one of the past fifty years, was that in each of them some, and in a number of cases many, had professed to accept Christ, and had since, by their changed lives, demonstrated that their conversions were real.

As part of the activities on that special and well-attended meeting of the Mission William Maxwell read a poem which he had composed to mark the occasion. He called it his Jubilee Ode.

Our citizens with pride look back
Along these fifty years,
Where progress marks her shining track,
And enterprise has not been slack
'Mong eager pioneers.
But where had many a modern pile
Found base its fabric to sustain,
Had not united art and toil
Claimed solid earth, as rightful spoil
Of conquest o'er the sea's domain?

And who can say how much that's best
And noblest in our city life,
Is due to half a century's strife
Where faith has oft been sorely pressed?
How oft our mission has made good,
Where all had else been desolate,
A rampart 'gainst the rising flood,
A foothold for the fear of God,
Who, who shall estimate?

The coming day shall tell,
Eternity alone declare,
How many heirs of hell,
Now raised where endless anthems swell,
Had sunk in darkness and despair
But for the Missionary's care.

Oft has the deadly plague been stayed
In hearts and lives of old and young,
As 'twixt the living and the dead
His prayers like smoking censers swung.
The hopeless, cheerless home became
The house of God, the gate of heaven,
As souls were filled with holy flame,
And voices blessed the Saviour's name
For joy of sin forgiven.

O happy toil, howe'er obscure,
By which he finds the fallen ones
And from the dunghill lifts the poor,
Erecting golden gates of praise
Amid salvation's bulwarks strong!
For this, O Lord, our hearts we raise,
Our efforts and our prayers prolong.
O let Thy sevenfold blessing be
The crown of this our jubilee,
The burden of our ceaseless song.

This poem summarised the worth of the work of the Mission, which continued to advance as before, but another special meeting of their subscribers was convened in April 1895 to address a very practical problem. Could they possibly change the title by which the organisation had been known for the greater part of the century?

It had become embarrassing.

The Belfast Town Mission had been operating in a city for well over six years. The time had come to do something about it.

Everyone present agreed that a change of name was necessary and the following resolution was passed unanimously:-

'Whereas Belfast, in A.D. 1888, having by Royal Charter been raised from the rank of a town to that of a city, and is now by common consent so designated : Be it resolved, that in the title of this Mission the word 'City' be substituted for that of 'Town', and that in future

the name of the Mission be 'The Belfast City Mission'
(formerly called 'The Belfast Town Mission')'

The Belfast *City* Mission had been born.

And Belfast city was still expanding, so the challenges to its newly
named mission with its unchanged objectives, were still increasing.

12

WHO CARES?

The final years of the nineteenth century witnessed the construction and subsequent launch of the biggest ship in the world at the time, in one of the biggest shipbuilding centres in the world at the time, Belfast.

By 1899 the workforce at Harland and Wolff's had risen to nine thousand, and many of those proud men joined an array of invited dignitaries on January 14 to see the **Oceanic**, the longest and most elegant ship ever built until then, take to the water.

A carnival atmosphere surrounded the launch.

Special excursion trains had brought a horde of visitors to the city. Shipbuilding experts from Britain, Germany and distant America had gathered to watch as the graceful giant glided down the slipway.

It was all over in a matter of seconds. Cheers rang out from the thousands of spectators as the **Oceanic** hit the Lagan in a great shower of spray drenching some of the more adventurous would-be photographers with their cumbersome equipment on the quayside.

Many of those watching the launch of the streamlined vessel with her two slim funnels were men who had been visited in their homes by the agents of the Belfast City Mission. The continued expansion of the heavy engineering industry in Belfast had attracted hundreds more families into the city and by 1899 there were twenty-four missionaries working amongst the steadily increasing population.

Recognising that huge numbers of people congregated every day to work in the city's many and often massive, workshops, factories and mills, the Mission introduced a new element of outreach to its range of activities, in the closing decade of the century.

It was the lunch hour meeting.

These gatherings were held either on open ground or at the factory gate in favourable weather or in a suitable room in the establishment, with the consent of the management, at other times.

In some districts very few either troubled to stop outside or bothered to attend inside. The workforce appeared more interested in talking about gambling than listening to the Gospel. The missionaries were not discouraged, though, and persisted prayerfully in their work.

God heard their prayers and honoured their efforts. Gradually lives began to be touched.

One missionary had carried on his meeting regularly in a factory warehouse with a number of men who came every week. Then one day a 'regular' brought along a workmate who confessed to never having been in a place of religious worship of any sort from his wedding twenty-eight years before.

He had been a habitual drunkard, but after having come to the lunch-hour meeting in the warehouse on a number of occasions he was alerted to the consequences of his sin. On learning of the provision made for his salvation in the death of Christ, he became a Christian. The tremendous change that took place in his life in the days and months following his conversion proved a continual source of wonder to all who knew him.

There were times, too, on pleasant summer days, and in other areas, when sizeable crowds lingered around to hear the message from the missionary, and were given tracts, which many promised to read. One agent was thrilled to report the interest shown by the workers of a large foundry in his district, in the open-air services at the gate. The men often stood around in hundreds listening to the short, pointed messages and some of them came forward as anxious enquirers. In many such cases when the missionary or someone assisting him had spoken to these men, they were led to the Saviour, standing in the street!

Conscious of the need to reach out into other parts of the city, and possibly having heard reports of successful campaigns under canvas across the province, in May 1898 the Mission committee purchased a large tent for use during the summer months.

The entire cost of the tent, fifty-seven pounds ten shillings, was raised by donations from interested individuals and business establishments.

The new tent was erected on land beside the Gasworks and meetings held every night for six weeks. This proved very worthwhile, for a number of people who had no church connections came along out of curiosity, and many were saved. One man, who had been addicted to drink for about ten years, and who had attempted, more that once, to take his own life, came to the tent, and trusted in Christ for salvation.

After that first year the Belfast City Mission tent was used in various locations across the city every summer.

In 1899 one missionary reported, 'Some people came to the tent meetings who could not be induced to attend any meeting previously. Indeed we could hardly accommodate all who came, the average attendance for 3 weeks being 340 nightly. The audiences were largely composed of working men of the neighbourhood, many of them most careless, and several of whom profess to have found salvation.'

In spite of these newer approaches to evangelism, the greater proportion of each missionary's time still continued to be taken up with visiting in the homes around his district. This remained the core element of the work for it was in doing this that he made contact with residents who didn't attend church and who had no interest in the Gospel.

Local Christians often suggested people who, because of a specific set of circumstances in their lives, would benefit from a visit by the City missionary.

Samuel, one of the agents, had a difficult, but ultimately rewarding series of experiences when this happened to him.

Late one summer Sunday evening, just as he was setting off for home after his final open-air service of the day, Samuel was approached by a lady who asked him to visit James, a sick man who lived in her street. She was concerned about him but warned Samuel that he had a foul tongue, a foul temper and no great love for Christians or indeed anything or anybody connected with religion.

A few days later Samuel called to see James and found that he had company. There were four other men present and the missionary was soon to discover that all five crammed into the tiny living room were bitterly antagonistic to both God and the Gospel.

When Samuel told James, whom he had come specifically to visit, that he was from the City Mission the householder exploded in a torrent of rage.

"I don't want anything to do with you or your religion!" he shouted, in an attempt to both impress his cronies and menace the missionary. "And if you don't get out I will put you out!"

Samuel was not to be intimidated, though, and had no notion of leaving. He wasn't going willingly, for he believed God wanted him to speak to these men.

He began by introducing topics of local interest but soon found him on the receiving end of a tirade of abusive language against all ministers, missionaries and Christian workers, of each and every denomination. They were hypocrites, every last one of them, according to these bitter men.

When the outburst had subsided Samuel began to ask James some personal questions and discovered that he had once attended a Presbyterian Church but had long since turned his back on religion.

As they continued to talk, all James' friends filed out one by one, leaving Samuel and his non-too welcoming host alone.

After offering an instant prayer for guidance, the missionary went on to explain the truth of the Gospel of redeeming grace to the man who had initially been so resistant. He then quoted the twenty-third Psalm and suggested that they should pray together.

Much to Samuel's surprise James slid down on his knees beside him and when they rose, a few minutes later, tears were running down his cheeks.

God had used the quoting of the familiar Psalm to awaken happy memories of childhood days and better, less bitter, feelings in James' mind. Then, after some further discussion, James opened his closed and hardened heart to the Lord.

Two days later Samuel called to see the new convert and was shocked to discover that he had passed away and the house was full of James' infidel friends. The missionary asked permission to pray, and after a brief session of hurried whispering among the relatives, some of whom knew Samuel, permission was granted. Seizing his opportunity, he commended the grieving family to God, and in thanking Him for James' recent conversion took care to incorporate the elements of the Gospel message in his prayer.

Some weeks later, one of the men who had been present at the wake when Samuel prayed turned up at his Sunday evening service and listened with interest as the Word was spoken. He continued to attend and eventually trusted in Christ.

What a harvest from one visit, suggested by a lady some three or four months before.

But what a struggle it had been at first!

What patience and persistence had been required!

The declaration of war between Britain and the Boers in an outpost of the empire on October 11, 1899, sent many young men rushing to join up. The prospect of an all expenses paid trip to sunny South Africa to fight for their country seemed too good an opportunity to miss, and within weeks many of Belfast's finest young men were on the high seas, heading south.

This Boer War, however, did not prove to be the picnic in the sun that many had anticipated. When news reached home of one defeat after another, and of much loss of life, many homes in Belfast were plunged into mourning for sons who had kissed mothers and girlfriends goodbye with such carefree abandon, but who wouldn't be coming back.

So in the early months of 1900 the agents of the Belfast City Mission found themselves fulfilling yet another role. There were so many homes to be visited, so many heart-broken relatives to be comforted, and so many people who needed to be told of the consolation which is only to be found in Christ.

The report for the year in which the Boer War began, 1899, opened with a comparison of the physical war far away which was on the minds of many, and the spiritual war at home which had escaped the notice of most. It stated,

'The present war in South Africa, with its costly sacrifices and far-reaching issues, has evoked a profound sensation throughout our Empire. The enthusiastic farewells to our departing soldiers, the absorbing interest with which the fortunes of war have been followed and the eager volunteering for active service, testify to the vast importance of the conflict.

A warfare of a different order, involving more momentous issues to thousands in this city, has been carried on by your Mission during another year. In the contest between light and darkness, virtue and vice, heaven and hell, we have had our share in the triumphs and defeats. Many of our operations have figured but little in the public eye, and our moral victories are known to but few besides those more immediately concerned...'

In a sense it was true. It was a minute percentage of the population of the city of Belfast who knew, or cared, about the little children who had come to Jesus in the Sabbath Schools, foundry men or mill workers who had trusted in Christ in the street outside their factory gates, drunkards whose lives and souls were saved in a tent somewhere, or people like James who had wept their way to repentance at their own fireside.

The people themselves knew, however, and so did the missionaries who had persevered in teaching and preaching the Gospel despite frequent discouragements.

Above all, the Lord knew, and He cared. And that was all that mattered.

It was His war. He had won the deciding battle over sin when He cried, 'It is finished!' on the cross.

Those who had signed up to fight for Him were carrying on the conflict in His Name, winning some battles, losing others.

It was reassuring, though, to know that He understood their struggles.

And cared.

13

WORLD LEADER

On the face of it, Belfast had begun to buzz.

The first decade of the twentieth century was a period of continuing industrial and economic growth against a backdrop of political discontent fuelled by the Home Rule issue, which hadn't gone away. And wasn't likely to, either.

By 1902 Belfast could boast of having the largest shipyard in the world, in Harland and Wolff's and the world's largest linen factory in the York Street Flax Spinning and Weaving Company. It also laid claim to the world's biggest ropeworks, tobacco factory, dry dock and mineral water factory.

On Tuesday, December 5, 1905, the first electric trams began operating on the streets of Belfast, carrying passengers any distance, on any route, for sixpence. The *Northern Whig* reported that 'Horse Traction died last night in the city, having lagged superfluously on the scene for the past five years...'

Then in 1906 the magnificent new building, the City Hall, resplendent in its Portland stone and with its green domes, was opened in Donegall Square.

Belfast appeared to both booming and beautiful.

But was it?

The missionary saw a different side to city life on his daily tramp around the streets. Away from the housing developments of the well-to-do that were continuing to gobble up green fields northwards into County Antrim and southwards into County Down, they still worked among the dwellings of the poor. And one of the biggest problems they encountered in such homes was drunkenness, which often resulted in domestic violence.

David Armstrong reported a tragic situation that he came across one day in the course of his visitation.

On entering a home at the invitation of what he took to be a girl's voice from inside, he was absolutely shocked to find the body of a three year-old boy lying stiff and cold in death on a heap of rags in the corner of the room. The father was in another corner totally intoxicated. There was no mother figure to be seen. David was later to discover that she had died three months earlier from alcohol poisoning. A lad of about seventeen lay slumped over a chair, hopelessly drunk.

"What happened to the wee boy?" David enquired of the only person in the room whom he deemed sober enough to give him a lucid reply. She was a thirteen-year old girl sitting on the floor with her back propped against the wall with the rags that she would have called clothes pulled tightly around her, terrified, and staring into space.

"He fell off a ladder out in the street two days ago, and a man brought him round here. I think he is dead now," came the tearful reply. "We have no money and I don't know what to do."

No doubt David did know what to do, though, and he would have contacted the different agencies required to resolve the situation.

It was an uphill, and often seemingly losing battle, against the havoc and hurt caused by habitual excessive drinking.

There were also, though, occasional flashes of hope that pierced the deepening darkness all around.

One afternoon Thomas Clokey, a City missionary, heard a voice calling after him as he was visiting systematically from door to door down a street in his district.

"Sir," came the call. "Sir, can I speak to you?"

When he turned round to see where the voice was coming from Thomas's attention was immediately attracted to a woman in her late twenties. She was hurrying up the street, her long hair blowing every way in the wind.

In less than a minute she had caught up with the missionary who had stopped on hearing her request. It was quite a pleasant change to have someone actually wanting to speak to him. In his work it usually fell to him to make the initial approach.

"I would like to thank you, sir," she burst out breathlessly, her face aglow whether from her recent exertions or from the genuine joy that was bubbling up within her. "You have worked wonders on my husband. He is a changed man."

"And who is your husband?" Thomas asked, his curiosity aroused.

When she told him her husband's name, Thomas said, "It wasn't me who changed him, it was God. Hugh came to some of my meetings and signed the pledge, but more importantly he also trusted in Christ. That's what made the difference."

"Oh I know, I know!" the young mother went on. "It is wonderful in our house now. Hugh reads the Bible and prays every day and we have money to buy things."

She paused, and then moving a step closer and dropping her voice to little more than a whisper, said, "And he doesn't hit me and the children any more!"

That was just one of a number of the triumphs of the Gospel in what the Mission secretary often designated in his reports as 'Dealing With The Drink.'

In the spring of 1903 Dr. R. A. Torrey and his choir leader Mr. Charles Alexander visited Belfast to conduct a number of meetings at various venues across the city. This created a considerable interest among and impact upon many who would not normally have been churchgoers, and the city missionaries took the opportunity to invite and accompany people from their districts to the services. The value of this visit, like those of D. L. Moody on previous occasions, was that it created a sense of spiritual awakening, which proved productive in the months and years that were to follow.

The Mission report for that year stated ,

'The influence of the Torrey-Alexander Mission made itself felt in many districts in the awakening of the careless to anxiety and decision and the imparting of fresh zeal and devotion to Sabbath School teachers and other helpers of the Missionaries. The happy effects are still evident more especially among the young, and in the greater readiness of many of the people to entertain the subject of personal salvation'.

The annual report each year in the early1900's referred, as this one did, to the growth and value of the work amongst the young, both in the Sabbath Schools and the Bible Class for Young People on a weeknight.

Most districts had two Sabbath Schools, one in the morning and another, usually much larger, in the afternoon, often in two different halls or schoolrooms in the area. In the Dee Street area of east Belfast, and in Beechpark Mission Hall there were three per Sabbath, one in the morning and two others in the afternoon.

In 1908 there were 42 Sabbath Schools in which more than 350 regular teachers instructed well over 5000 children in the Word of God every Sunday across the city.

Each missionary was responsible for arranging a Bible Class for young people in their teens and early twenties once a week and these meetings were also well attended. The largest of these was in the Beersbridge Road Schoolroom where Samuel Spence often spoke to over a hundred every week. The classes in Comber Street and in the New Lodge Road district had between eighty and a hundred coming on a regular basis, as well.

Statistics may be of natural interest but they are of no eternal significance whatever, however. It was what happened in the Sabbath Schools and Bible Classes that was of any lasting importance for God and forever.

Many children and young adults came to know Christ as Saviour through the consistent presentation of the Gospel by dedicated Sabbath School teachers and Bible Class leaders.

When Robert Barkley was tidying up one Thursday evening after his Bible Class in Donegall Road Schoolroom he noticed that three lads seemed in no hurry to go home. They kept dallying around.

Eventually one of them approached Robert and asked if they could talk to him about something.

When the missionary enquired what they wanted another told him that he would like to trust in Jesus and his companions said something the same. Robert was delighted to sit down with the trio around him, and opening his Bible he pointed them to Jesus, the Way, the Truth and the Life. One boy began to weep as the conversation progressed, and within half an hour all three had come to Christ for salvation.

The three lads stayed with Robert, still talking, as he was locking the outside door. Suddenly the lad who had made the initial request for an interview with the missionary pulled a packet of cigarettes from his pocket, screwed them up and threw them away.

"I won't have much need of those any more," he remarked emphatically.

A middle aged woman whom Ernest Barr had never met before came to his evening service in Jersey Street Schoolroom one Sunday. On the way out she said to the missionary, "My daughter Sally," and she paused to nod at a girl standing behind her, "has been pestering me to come here for weeks. I promised her I would come for since she has been converted at your Bible Class a month or two ago she has been a different girl to have about the house. She even sits and reads her Bible before going out to work in the morning!"

Sally stood clutching that Bible and smiling broadly as she listened to her mother's description of her change of heart and life.

William Walker from Roden Street was pleased at the number of chapters of the scriptures that some of the children in the Sabbath School had been able to commit to memory, but he took special encouragement from the progress Thomas was making in spiritual matters.

This Thomas was an intelligent young man who had been saved in the Sabbath School as a child and had moved on to take charge of a large class of lively boys. William praised God for Thomas for not only had he tamed a turbulent class that nobody else seemed to have been able to manage, but he had also led some of its most disruptive members to faith in Christ.

The Mission was seeing results for God in almost all of its activities but these were small when compared to the need around.

The annual report for 1907 reiterated the aim of having a missionary to serve every house in the city but repeated the problem that had dogged development for so many decades. It was the lack of funds.

'We are short of workers because we are short of money,' it confessed, 'but there is another reason. The salaries of our agents are not sufficiently remunerative compared with what they would be receiving in other directions.'

It was happening again.

In 1900 there had been twenty-four full time missionaries but by 1907 that had dropped back to twenty. Men who had either retired or passed on to be with the Lord hadn't been replaced.

That annual meeting in the Assembly Hall in Fisherwick Place had drawn the largest crowd ever to attend such a meeting of the Mission, and this was no doubt due, at least in part, to the fact that the invited speaker that year was the well-known evangelist, Gipsy Smith.

During his address the preacher, who was renowned for his forthrightness, made a couple of suggestions for what he described as a 'great aggressive movement for the evangelisation of the people of Belfast.'

'If Presbyterians next Sabbath, instead of going to church, would go to the corner of the street with their parson and elders and office bearers, and hold an open air meeting, they would do more good than they ever could by sitting inside four walls," he proclaimed.

Then looking directly down at his audience he asked, "Do you people believe that?"

"Yes," came the echoing reply from all over the hall.

"Well then, why don't you do it?" Gipsy Smith went on to challenge them.

Everybody laughed, but there is no record of any church ever having taken him up on his suggestion.

He was equally frank with them on the matter of finance.

"Your total income for the work of the Mission for last year was £1,700, but what is that when measured against the wealth of Belfast Presbyterianism?" he enquired. "Why, in some quarters they would spend as much as that on one political meeting! The Church of God cannot save the slums on the cheap. When those with means begin to show as much concern for a man's soul as they do for his vote, then, and not until then, will the masses get saved."

It was hard-hitting stuff.

Gipsy Smith then went on to advance a very practical idea.

"Why don't some of you businessmen put an amount of money into the bank and say to one or two of the men who are labouring in your area, doing what you could be doing for Christ's sake, 'I will spare you the worry of finance. You go ahead and carry on with your work. I will meet your expenses."

What he was suggesting was in effect spiritual sponsorship, and could have been most beneficial to the spread of the Gospel and the financial position of the Mission.

With the treasurer's report for the following year, 1908, showing that the Mission's income had increased by just over £100 in the twelve-month period it is most likely that the address, which had touched peoples' hearts, hadn't actually gone deep enough to touch their pockets or their purses.

Or at least not yet.

As the work of the Mission went on as usual for years reaching out into the homes of the poor with the riches of the Gospel of grace the political tensions continued to increase in both the province of Ulster and the city of Belfast.

In September 1912, Lord Carson signed the Covenant in the City Hall and over 470,000 people followed his lead in the days that followed. These were men and women who wished to retain their 'position of equal citizenship in the united Kingdom' and who pledged themselves to 'use all means which may be found necessary to defeat the present conspiracy to set up Home Rule Parliament in Ireland'.

A huge cloud of gloom had descended on the city in April of that same year with the loss of the White Star's luxury liner 'Titanic' after it struck an iceberg in the North Atlantic. 1,490 passengers and crew had lost their lives in that disaster. It seemed that everybody in the city was affected in some way, from bewildered shipyard workers who had been so proud of their handiwork and devastated at its loss, to city missionaries who had the opportunity to comfort some of those bereaved and warn others of the brevity and uncertainty of this life.

The rising tide of opposition to the concept of Home Rule in the Province and the possibility of a civil war over the issue began to chill many minds and inflame many passions as 1912 slid into 1913. A sense of agitation and aggravation had gripped the city.

And nobody could have predicted what lay just up ahead.

14

BROKEN HOMES AND BLEEDING HEARTS

Although money was tight in the Mission the committee decided to take a forward step of faith and purchase 'a commodious Hall' in Cuba Street, off the Newtownards Road when this property came on the market in 1911.

After protracted negotiations conducted by an able businessman on the committee the Hall, with two adjoining dwelling houses, was procured for £400.

It was amazing the effect that purchase had on the pockets and purses of hitherto more reticent benefactors. Perhaps it was the ability to see something practical and permanent as opposed to imagining something spiritual and ethereal that inspired a number of donors, but in the space of four months £300 had been received towards its purchase.

Following the acquisition of the Hall in Cuba Street, the Belfast City Mission was to have a second Hall built specifically for its own use the next year.

Mr. James Cuthbert, who had been for years a member of the Mission's Management Committee, purchased a piece of ground and had a Hall built on it in Lord Street, in the Ballymacarret district of the city. He not only erected, but also completely furnished this building at a total cost of £800.

Both these halls were pressed into use as soon as possible and within weeks of its opening the Sabbath School in Lord Street was completely packing the new building. The financial investment in the purchase of these properties had begun to show an immediate and profitable spiritual return.

Perhaps Gipsy Smith's challenge to the Christian men and women of means in the city hadn't fallen on deaf ears after all!

Mr. William Maxwell, the Mission's first permanent secretary and financial agent was forced to resign his position in 1913 owing to failing health. He had graced the office for twenty-four years and in that time the Mission had made many advances. William Maxwell had been a capable and respected administrator and his prowess with the pen, both in the compiling of reports and the composing of poetry had often proved inspirational to flagging spirits. Above all he had been a person with a sincere love for God and the work of the Mission and his advice, based on years of experience, was always greatly appreciated.

His successor, Mr. Francis Mulligan, had been, like Mr. Maxwell, a city missionary himself before being appointed to the position of secretary and financial Agent in the latter half of 1913. Years of service on the ground in the McClure Street district had provided him with valuable background knowledge of the practicalities of the work and he 'entered on the duties of his office with the goodwill and esteem of the entire committee'.

By 1914 there were again twenty-three agents working diligently for God in the streets and lanes of the city. This was encouraging. Sinister developments in local and world events, however, were less heartening.

The dark clouds of political uncertainty that had been thickening over Ireland had begun to spread across Europe and around the world, blocking out the rays of the sun of hope for many.

In the spring of that year political strife had reached a state of frenzy across the island of Ireland. Both Unionists and Nationalists had begun to drill and arm with gunrunning and volunteer parades providing one sensational headline after another. Then, just when it seemed that civil war was only a matter of days, or at the most, weeks away, the trouble at home was eclipsed by the outbreak of war in Europe.

On August 1 Germany declared war on Russia and three days later Britain was at war with Germany. Once again there was a rush to join the army to serve King and country, and this was a rush in which the men of Belfast and Ulster were not afraid to take the lead. Some of them had been training in arms for years and responded to the call of duty with alacrity. Heartbreaking scenes of departure became familiar features of railway stations across the province once again as noble young men boarded trains to be transported to the port of Belfast where they joined others from the city on the quays to await embarkation to the front.

In less than a year the horror of a World War at sea and on land had claimed the lives of countless victims. Men's hearts began failing them for fear as they were forced to contemplate the terror which had been unleashed on a relatively unsuspecting and unprepared world.

People had been confronted with the spectre of wholesale slaughter on an unprecedented scale and had been compelled to consider the implications of impending death and the judgement of God.

When presenting his report of the various activities of the Mission during 1915 Rev. Dr. Montgomery referred to the inevitable effect of a war of such magnitude in the homes of the residents, and on the ministry of the missionaries, in their home city.

'Amid events, unparalleled in the annals of history,' he began, 'when to many the very foundations seem to be shaken, your agents have been at work, and ever rejoicing in the triumphs of the Cross and the message it has for the broken and bleeding hearts of men. They have visited the shadowed homes of the city with their war toll of sorrowing parents, widows, and fatherless children. They have come into contact with hearts ploughed by bereavement and stricken with the sense of irreparable loss.

In all such homes the Gospel messenger has been a welcome visitor, and never in the past were his calls more highly appreciated or productive of so much good as in these trying times. All reports go to show that the people are not only thinking more deeply today, but they evince a readiness to speak freely about the things that belong to their eternal peace.'

Having outlined the role of the missionaries in bringing a message of consolation into the hurting homes of the city during that year of war Dr. Montgomery then went on to say that many men associated with the Mission had enlisted and were currently serving with the forces overseas.

One can almost imagine the gentlemanly air of patriotic pride suffused with a deep sense of personal loss with which he would continue,

'It is gratifying to record that in response to our country's call the men associated with our Mission have nobly responded. The City Mission Honour Roll stands at the high figure of over 800. Some of these brave men have fallen on the stricken field and many have been wounded, while the others are still fighting by land and sea for the protection of their King and fatherland and the larger liberty. Our prayer is that God will be very gracious to each of them, and so far as it is in accordance with His divine purpose, cover their heads in the day of battle.'

As the war raged in the battlefields of the world the city missionaries continued in the battle against sin and evil in the homes and halls of their districts. Many of them found people happy to have the Word of God read in their homes and genuine enquiries about fathers, sons or brothers engaged in active military service often led to opportunities to comfort those whose loved ones had been killed or wounded, or openings to present the need of salvation.

In May 1915 Billy Spence, a converted street boxer, was invited to conduct a fortnight's meetings in one of the City Mission Halls. Big crowds attended, some out of curiosity, others out of genuine interest. At the end of the two-week period eleven people had come to Christ. The missionary in that area was pleased at this wave of blessing, for not only were these converts continuing to live consistent and changed lives, but some of them had become active in helping him in various aspects of the work.

The month of June that year was very warm and sunny and in John Cunningham's city centre district an open-air meeting was held every evening in a different location. One evening it could have been Great Victoria Street, the next it was perhaps Sandy Row, and then another evening the meeting could have been in Blythe Street or one of the other little streets running off it.

Many people who could never have been persuaded to enter a church building stood around or sat on windowsills in the pleasant evening sunshine and listened to the good news of the Gospel. Then when the missionary and those helping him mingled with the bystanders or spoke to the windowsill sitters afterwards they were delighted to be able to point a few of them to the Lord.

John noticed a man who seemed to turn up at the open-airs, perhaps three or four nights a week, wherever they were held across the district.

Later in the year that same man arrived in the Sunday evening service in Linfield Street Schoolroom. Having listened intently to the preaching he said to John on the way out, "I want to talk to you about this salvation."

The missionary was only too glad to comply with such a request and spent some time with the Bible explaining the way of salvation. The man appeared confused, even frustrated, by the simplicity of the message on that first evening. A few weeks later, though, he told John that he had put his faith in Jesus. From that time on he became a most regular supporter of all the meetings in Linfield Street.

God was at work in the city.

Deep in the shadow of war people were coming to Him.

The next year, 1916, was a tragic year for Belfast, and indeed the province of Ulster.

The Easter Rising in Dublin rekindled the Home Rule controversy in the minds of many and there were successive setbacks for the Allies in the war on both land and sea. Hopes of a turnaround in the fortunes of the forces rested on the plans for a massive offensive on the River Somme in the summer time.

At the outbreak of war, two years before, Lord Carson had urged the members of the Ulster Volunteer Force to 'join the army and help save your country'. Following his command that band of men had been swept, almost completely, into the 36th (Ulster) Division of the British Army. In May 1915 the Division had paraded proudly past the front of Belfast City Hall to the ringing cheers of the spectators who lined the pavements four and five deep.

It was this same Division, however, some fourteen months later, on July 1, 1916, that was chosen to spearhead the attack on the German lines, in what everyone hoped would be a decisive Battle at the Somme.

But things went disastrously wrong.

The horror of that day lived in the minds of the few who survived, often disabled or disfigured, to their dying day.

The Ulster Division had moved forward out of the safety of their trenches at half past seven in the morning under cover of a smoke screen and also an early morning mist. As they advanced, orderly row upon orderly row, these brave men became easy targets for enemy fire. Wave after wave of them were mown down, yet those remaining persisted in pushing valiantly forward. They succeeded in reaching and overwhelming some of the German front lines and just when it seemed that they had won a momentous victory they began to be bombarded by ceaseless shelling from behind their own lines. The 36th Division had made such rapid advances that they had reached the enemy lines at least ten minutes before that had been considered possible and were caught up in so-called 'friendly fire'.

A pathetic letter, which Private Herbie Beattie wrote to his mother following that awful battle, revealed something of the unspeakable horror of the situation. Having told her that 'there is not another Grosvenor Road fellow left but myself' he described how they had been 'tramping over the dead' and concluded that 'if hell is any worse I would not like to go to it'.

It had been horrendous.

On that first day of the Battle of the Somme, 5,500 men of the Ulster Division had been either killed or wounded.

When news of this disaster broke in Ulster a black blanket of gloom descended on the province. Many homes across the city of Belfast had been affected. It seemed as though everyone in that community had either lost a relative at the Somme, or knew somebody else who had.

On July 12 the traditional parades were voluntarily abandoned. As the clocks struck twelve noon all traffic in the streets of Belfast came to a stop. Business premises were closed up and public courts adjourned. Blinds were drawn.

The city was in mourning for its sons.

Throughout the month of July the Belfast City missionaries joined with the ministers and leaders of other denominations in seeking to bring succour to the sorrowing. In many of the districts almost every street had at least one house which had been overcome with grief following the decimation of the Ulster division.

This ministry to the sorrowing carried on well into the winter with Missionaries finding themselves welcome to read the Scriptures and pray in houses where they had never previously been across the doorstep. Continued Christian care and compassion in a tragic set of circumstances often bore fruit in salvation and in families joining, or returning to, a local church.

The Mission report for the year 1916 included a unique and unusual insertion demonstrating the prominent place which the ongoing war occupied in the minds of everyone. It highlighted the part played by those associated with the Mission both at home and on the battlefield. It said,

> 'Our Mission and the War
> From all our Mission districts brave men have gone forth at the call of King and country to serve on land and sea in connection with the present war. It has been the privilege of the missionaries to visit in the homes of these gallant men, advising and helping their wives and children and other relatives and offering their prayerful sympathy when sad news comes to hand telling of dear ones who have made the ultimate sacrifice.'

In stark contrast to the disturbing news of loss of human life in the war there was some good news on the advancement of the mission work in Belfast. That year five generous friends of the Mission had combined to fund the appointment of an additional missionary to work in a needy development area which up until then had been unreached by the Mission through lack of finance.

Whether this act of munificence was inspired at the suggestion of Gipsy Smith, by the evolving human anguish of the war, or through a sincere love for God and a care for the careless and churchless citizens of Belfast, it would be impossible to tell. Perhaps it was a mixture of all three.

Whatever the reason, the fact remained that the spiritual struggle against sin and wickedness, drunkenness and degradation, being fought in the homes and streets, the Sabbath Schools and Mission Halls of the city, was still continuing.

And reinforcements had been summoned.

15

COME QUICKLY MISTER!

Although the cessation of hostilities in World War I on November 11, 1918, brought with it a sense of relief to the countries involved it did not bring peace to the streets of Belfast. The Home Rule question had been shelved for the duration of the War, but it hadn't been resolved, and political unrest soon began again.

Then a serious outbreak of influenza brought debilitating illness, and in some cases death, to homes that had escaped bereavement during the war years.

The 'flu epidemic increased the workload, but also the openings to contact the hitherto uncontacted, for the City missionaries. When the illness was at its most widespread in the winter of 1918–19 David Boyd, the missionary for the York Street and Docks area of the city found himself conducting up to twelve funerals in the week and visiting homes where there were eight and nine people all ill at the same time.

Within the space of a year the 'flu epidemic had subsided, however, but the political instability hadn't. Tensions increased. Death on the streets became a feature of city life once more.

In December 1920 it was agreed in Westminster that the six northeastern counties of Ireland should be granted Home Rule, with their own Parliament based in Belfast. This didn't satisfy every shade of opinion and the trouble continued.

King George V came to address the state opening of the new Northern Ireland Parliament in the City Hall in June 1921 against a backcloth of conflict. Seven people had been killed in rioting in the city just ten days before he stepped ashore at the docks and was driven up High Street and along Donegall Place surrounded by a tight security cordon.

The situation worsened. The winter of 1921–22 was marked by attack and counter attack with each faction accusing the other of 'starting it'. When it came to the summer of 1922 more than 450 people had lost their lives on the streets of Belfast in two years of sporadic violence.

This was the setting in which the agents of the Belfast City Mission carried on their work for the Lord, endeavouring to look away from themselves and the aggro all around and 'unto Jesus, the Author and Finisher' of their faith.

In the summer of 1921, with people frightened to leave their homes to come to the meetings of the Mission in some of the more disturbed districts the management committee became burdened for the state of the city and the future of the Mission's many outreach and pastoral interests. This mounting concern spurred them into action and their first step was to 'carry everything to God in prayer'.

Special prayer meetings were held in the Mission office in Fisherwick Place at nine o'clock every morning for two weeks. These were well attended as they afforded all those with an interest in the Mission, and many other committed Christians, the opportunity to pray earnestly for political peace and spiritual revival in the city.

God heard and answered those fervent prayers of his anxious people in a marvellous way. In his report for that year, Dr. Montgomery admitted that 'the success and blessing which have attended the missionaries' efforts during the past year have surpassed our highest hopes and rebuked our unbelief. God heard our prayer and manifested his power in such a way that the whole work of the Mission has been completely transformed. Without any special effort the attendances at meetings and Bible Classes greatly increased, and anxious ones remained behind at the close of almost every meeting to seek the Saviour. This movement has spread all over the city. There is scarcely a district which has not shared in the blessing. In some areas large numbers received the Saviour, and whole families have been converted and the life of the home blessed and transformed.'

That fruitful year, 1921, saw the commencement of a period when God moved in a remarkable manner in the city of Belfast and called many seeking souls to Himself.

Religious fervour became evident in the churches and halls once more, despite the political fanaticism all around.

The visit of Mr. William P. Nicholson to the city in 1922 saw packed churches and thousands of conversions.

One of the evangelist's first Gospel campaigns was in February of that year in the Albert Hall, at the invitation of the Shankill Road Mission. The troubles were at their height at that time and up to three thousand people disregarded the danger from flying bullets and exploding bombs every night, just to hear the Word of God.

Hundreds were saved in that mission and then Mr. Nicholson moved across the city to Newington Presbyterian Church on the Limestone Road and here again capacity crowds were recorded. On some evenings 2000 people were jammed and crammed into every available nook and cranny in the building, and hundreds were saved as the mission progressed.

In the early autumn of 1922 the fiery evangelist returned to the city conducting missions in Sandy Row and in the biggest Presbyterian Church in Belfast, St. Enoch's, where every seat in the building was taken an hour before the meeting, every night. Then Mr. Nicholson conducted further packed out campaigns in east Belfast. Everywhere he went huge crowds followed him, attracted by his unorthodox style, entertained by his scathing attacks on ineffective churches, but ultimately arrested by the sense of the presence of God that accompanied his preaching.

Poor people couldn't afford to take the tram across the city to the Nicholson meetings, but having heard of souls saved and lives transformed in other areas, they could stop at an open-air meeting conducted by a city missionary to hear what this Gospel was all about. And many did. Missionaries had no difficulty, either, in persuading people to attend the mission meetings in their hall.

Thousands turned to the Lord in the services conducted by W.P. Nicholson and hundreds more were reached by the efforts of the Belfast City Mission. All these new converts had to be instructed in Christian living and this led to a significant increase in the numbers attending the Bible Classes run by the Mission.

An awakening was under way, and continued.

Early in 1923 La Marechale, the eldest daughter of General Booth, the founder of the Salvation Army, arrived in Belfast to hold a Gospel outreach campaign.

The novelty of hearing a woman, and a woman from such a spiritually famous family, preaching, proved attractive, and thousands flocked to hear her. In her case a most winsome appeal, a magnetic, caring personality, and a definite gift for dramatics were all used in an unmistakeable presentation of the message of salvation. And hundreds of those who thronged to hear her, often out of nothing more than curiosity, came face to face with the claims of Christ and trusted in Him as their Saviour.

The Belfast City Mission shared in the benefits of La Marechale's visit in much the same way as they had done with former missions down the years, in at least two ways. It inspired an increase in zeal amongst its members, but more importantly it created an atmosphere in which non-Christians could easily air and share their spiritual concerns.

In addition to the multiple conversions as a result of the series of Gospel campaigns which had so moved many in the city over two or three years, the consistent visitation of the City Missionaries to the homes in their districts also proved productive.

Many poor people found themselves in situations of real distress in 1924 when the effects of the commercial and industrial depression began to bite into the heart of what had become a commercial and industrial city, Belfast. The missionaries worked hard to alleviate the hardship occasioned by unemployment in many homes, but some of the other problems they encountered were caused by what had long since become the scourge of many working class families, an addiction to alcohol.

For example, one afternoon Alex Nimmo knocked on a door in a side street off the Woodstock Road and after a short interval a man with blood running down his face from a cut on his forehead came to answer it.

When he explained that he was from the Belfast City Mission and was visiting in the area the man invited him to come in. The bloodstained host entered the tiny living room a few steps ahead of Alex and he was greeted by a torrent of verbal abuse. Not to be outdone, and regardless of the presence of the missionary, the man of the house returned the abuse in a cascade of colourful language.

Alex had arrived right in the middle of a violent domestic dispute which had been, if the litter scattered around was anything to go by, accompanied by a flying missile or two. Both partners were, if not drunk, certainly well under the influence of alcohol.

Using soft words and a gentle approach Alex eventually managed to see the combatant couple both settled down and sitting down, and having asked permission read a short scripture passage and prayed briefly with them.

As he was about to leave the home the missionary invited the pair to a cottage meeting near to where they lived and they promised to go.

A week later Alex was pleased, if not slightly surprised, to find that they had kept their word, and they soon began to make regular appearances at the Sunday evening services in Ravenhill Road schoolroom.

They had only been attending for a few months when Alex pointed the wife to the Lord after a meeting and a short time later the husband became a Christian as well.

Alex was thrilled to witness the change in their lives and in their home and they often laughed with him when recalling the 'day of the big fight'!

In another incident William Lynas was in his home in Hatfield Street, off the Ormeau Road, and just preparing to go to bed when there was a loud, insistent knocking at his front door. When he opened it he found a girl of eight or nine years old standing on the footpath. She looked terrified.

"Come quickly mister!" she screamed without any attempt at introduction. Her voice rose to a shriek with an urgency driven by anxiety as she went on, "My daddy has come home drunk and he is beating my mummy all round the house! Oh, it's awful!"

Taking only half a minute to pull on a pair of shoes and grab an overcoat William followed the girl as she ran to another street and pushed her way into a house. The breathless missionary went in after her.

The beating had been abandoned but a very dishevelled pair were facing each other across a half-wrecked room.

The woman was crying.

William spent more than an hour with them, talking, calming, suggesting, and finally praying.

As he rose to go the father shook his hand and said, as coherently as he could, "With the help of God I won't be taking any more drink or backing any more horses."

Whether he kept those pledges or not William Lynas had no way of knowing, but he did begin to attend the mission meetings in McClure Street Schoolroom. Then two weeks later at the close of a meeting he trusted in Christ as his Saviour.

Before he left for home that night he held the missionary firmly by the hand yet again and declared, "I thank God for the night the wee girl brought you round to our house and you talked to us about Jesus."

The new convert then began to go to church every Sunday and he and his wife, who had also been saved, began to help with the work of the Mission. He told William one day, "We have been married fifteen years and we have never known anything about real happiness until now."

God was at work in Belfast in the 1920's, both in mission meetings that filled huge buildings to their utmost capacity and in humble homes in the network of side streets that fanned out all over the city.

Summarising his years with the Mission up until that period, John Coulter, an experienced missionary stated, 'At no time during the past sixteen and a half years has the tide of blessing risen so high. Meetings, Sunday Schools and Bible Classes have been crowded, and the revival spirit has pervaded all. Many of God's own people have been lifted to a higher plane of Christian living, and are now filled with a passion for souls. Sinners have been saved and backsliders restored. The work among the young men is growing steadily and is of a most encouraging character. The men who were led to Christ in the opening months of the year are growing in grace and are most anxious to gather the godless and careless men of the district into the 'Men's Own Meeting on a Sabbath afternoon.'

When introducing his report for 1925 Dr. Montgomery presented a more general view of what he described as the 'onward progress of the Belfast City Mission'.

He said that 'the work of the Mission is to Belfast as a cleansing stream passing through the waste and dark places, and wherever its operations extend lives are changed, homes are purified and souls are saved.'

It was wonderful!

The country had been hit by an industrial recession and yet the Belfast City Mission was riding on the crest of a wave of blessing.

And there would soon be something more for which all concerned would wish to render heartfelt praise to God.

They would soon have been reaching out to the poor of the city for a hundred years. Their centenary was fast approaching. It was thrilling to contemplate.

A century of service!

16

ONE HUNDRED NOT OUT

The plight of the poor in Belfast in 1927, when the City Mission was preparing to celebrate its centenary, had become desperate. By then the city, which had one-third of the population of Northern Ireland within its boundaries had 60,000 unemployed. This was half of the jobless figure for the entire province. Hardship abounded in the homes of the people with whom the agents of the Belfast City Mission had established a pattern of visitation.

Yet as they came together to mark their centenary the leaders of the Mission were constrained to praise God for His help and blessing in a remarkable way. In that year there were twenty-nine missionaries working in different districts across the city. The Mission had also received the gift of a suitable hall and had built two others each capable of seating over three hundred people. These were in Kimberly Street and on the Donegall Road. A further encouraging factor was that the Mission's financial position was healthier than it had ever been before.

The increase in financial support was due, at least in some measure, to the promotional efforts of Francis Mulligan, the Mission's secretary and financial agent. He had endeavoured to make the worth of the work widely known and during the 1920's annual incomes increased considerably. In addition to local giving through mission boxes in homes, a growing number of committed Christians became involved in helping fund an extra missionary to open up another district, or giving generously towards the cost of building the new mission halls across the city.

There was also a heightened awareness of the work of the Mission in Presbyterian Churches, not only in the greater Belfast area, but also across the province. Donations began to arrive in the office from rural congregations in such places as Kilraughts and Killymurris in County Antrim and urban congregations in Bangor and Ballynahinch in County Down, to name but a few. Employers in the city must also have recognised the value of the efforts of the mission to alleviate the misery of the poor for many of them began making regular annual donations in the 1920's. The two most generous firms for many years represented the two most prominent industries in city. One was James & T. Mackie, makers of textile machinery, from the heavy engineering sector, and the other was the York Street Flax Spinning Company from linen manufacture.

There had been many changes in Belfast during those first one hundred years of the Mission. When William Cochrane first visited the homes of the poor in the squalid lanes and courts, they were lit by candles. Years later paraffin lamps were hailed as a big advance and the gaslight which followed was simply wonderful. In 1927 many of the homes in the city were illuminated by a marvellous mystical power called electricity.   .

When the first agent of the Mission arrived in the town of Belfast he would probably have come by stagecoach. The trains which came later were so much faster and marginally more comfortable depending on whether one travelled in the first or third class carriages. The arrival of the motorcar in the early years of the new century was a significant development and then when the Wright Brothers pioneered powered flight people began to talk about a strange flying machine called an aeroplane.

The annual report for 1927, when presented, not only focussed on the work of that year but also summarised in a delightful, almost poetic manner, the spiritual achievements of the previous one hundred.

'Though one of the oldest of the evangelical and philanthropic agencies in the city,' it began, 'the Belfast City Mission still has the power of adapting itself to the needs of the people, and is grappling with the sins and sorrows of life so common in our midst. Since its inception it had demonstrated the value of persistent evangelistic work, and has done much to sweeten and elevate the life of the community.

When we realise that we are today celebrating the Centenary of the Mission, what a retrospect opens to our view!

One hundred years of patient plodding work.

One hundred years of personal dealing with men and women.

One hundred years of excavating among the wreckage as for hidden treasure.

One hundred years of bringing the Gospel to the lonely and desolate, to the sick and dying.

One hundred years of spreading the Gospel light in the dark places of the city.

One hundred years of Sabbath School work, winning the young as 'gems for His crown.'

What a retrospect!

Eternity alone will reveal its true value.'

Dr. Montgomery, who had presented so many annual reports, was unfortunately unable to attend the centenary celebration because of illness but he sent a message through his joint secretary, David Irwin. He said that he joined many in 'ascribing glory and honour and praise to the God who has watched over the fortunes of the Mission during its hundred years history.'

Having given thanks to God for the work done by the Mission, and declared that 'it was just as fitting an agent to bring the Gospel to the careless and non-Church-going of the city as it had been one hundred years ago,' he went on to make a very practical proposal. The time had come, he suggested, for 'the Christian people of the city and province to express their appreciation of the splendid work accomplished by launching a generous scheme for providing a retiring allowance for missionaries when they felt obliged to withdraw from active duty owing to advancing years.'

He commended the scheme he was proposing, 'in the Name of our Lord and Master.' It would be gratifying if the appeal would meet with 'a generous response, and that one of the results of the centenary proceedings would be the inauguration of a much-needed fund for the benefit of the men who have given their best to the work of the Mission.'

To mark the occasion the Mission committee produced a little pamphlet with a dual aim no doubt. This publication would highlight what had been achieved for God by the Mission's outreach to the poor of the city and thus increase both prayerful and financial support in years to come. It was entitled BELFAST CITY MISSION, and subtitled, One Hundred Years Spreading the Light of the Gospel in the City.

The facts about the mission which it enumerated are remarkable, and worth reproducing, as they record how far the Mission had developed since their sole agent had travelled into Belfast to commence his work, alone, a century before.

1   The aim of the Mission is the moral and spiritual welfare of the people.

2   Last year 67,628 visits were paid in the homes of the people; 11,894 were to the sick and dying; 1,981 to hospitals and institutions.

3   Last year 5,632 Gospel Meetings were held in Halls, Cottages, Factories and at Street Corners.

4   There are 40 Sabbath Schools under the auspices of the Mission, with 700 teachers and over 9,000 Scholars.

5   107 families were brought into Church connexion last year.

6   The Missionary whose district adjoins the Docks visited 831 Ships in port during the year.

7 Last year the Mission received the gift of a Mission Hall, and built two new ones.

8   A new book, entitled 'For Christ and Crown,' giving the history of the Mission since its inception, by Mr. R. M. Sibbett, is just published, and can be had from all booksellers, or at the City Mission Office. Price 3/6.

The special pamphlet also included photographs of the office-bearers and missionaries in 1927 and a poem praising God for the triumphs of the Gospel over one hundred years of Mission endeavour. This poem was composed by Mr. James Bell, a missionary in the Shankill Road district of the city, and sung by the choir at the centenary meeting.
James called it simply,

BELFAST CITY MISSION, 1827 –1927.

What thoughts of untold gladness
Hang o'er the vanished years,
The tale of sin and sadness
From memory disappears.
We think of souls immortal
Saved from the depths of woe,
Through men who sought, and prayed and wrought,
A hundred years ago.

'Twas but a little cloudlet,
No bigger than man's hand,
O'er city street and alley
By breath of heaven fanned.
In drops of glad refreshing
By pure and gentle flow,
It slaked the thirst, and saved the worst,
A hundred years ago.

And through the years revolving
The little cloudlet grew,
The city's sorrows solving
And bringing hopes anew
To those whose lives were shattered
And worsted in the fight.
To dying ones, to mothers' sons
It brought the Gospel light.

Still growing, ever growing,
The 'little cloud' has spread
In widening volume, showing
The pathway from the dead.
To Him be all the Glory
In all increasing flow,
Who lives again, Who died for men,
Long centuries ago.

The Belfast City Mission had seen much accomplished for God in its first hundred years. 'To Him be all the Glory' indeed.

And it wasn't finished yet either!

17

RECYCLED PEOPLE

Unemployment became an even more pressing problem in Belfast in the early 1930's. The economic decline had begun to affect both shipbuilding and linen manufacture in a significant way and many thousands were thrown out of work.

By 1932 there were 78,000 unemployed people in the city, and that year was the first for as long as most could remember in which not one single ship had been launched from the formerly bustling yards of Harland & Wolff.

Inadequate unemployment benefit left many homes in a state of starvation. Desperation fuelled by deprivation led to rioting on the streets. The Unemployed Workers' Committee summed up the situation in a terse statement. 'Hundreds and hundreds of people are absolutely destitute in this city,' they said. 'They are begging and borrowing like worms.'

The Presbyterian Churches in Belfast, concerned for the plight of many of the people in the poorer districts of the city, consulted a number of their ministers and the Board of the City Mission about the worsening state of affairs. They then combined to register their mounting anxiety by adopting the following resolution,

'We, the members of the Presbytery of Belfast, are deeply concerned about the widespread distress in our city, due to unemployment and the exhaustion in many cases of unemployment benefit. We are of the opinion that as a rule the grants that are being made to those who are entirely dependent on outdoor relief are inadequate to provide the barest necessities of life.'

The Committee, missionaries and volunteer workers of all ages in the Belfast City Mission responded very practically to the anguish all around them, as the report for 1932 would indicate. It states,

'The Committee desire to express their grateful thanks to the many friends who have helped them in the relief of distress, and also to the churches which have assisted by gifts of money, food and clothing.

The past year has been a trying time for the missionaries, many of those among whom they labour having become embittered, while others have almost lost hope through the long-continued unemployment and poverty. These combine to add to the difficulties of the mission worker. Nothing but the power of Him Who came to seek and to save that which was lost, and the joy of making known His salvation, could sustain them in this work.'

The very practical ministry of the missionaries in providing for those whom they found living well below the bread line often reaped a positive harvest, not only in the alleviation of the immediate distress but also in seeing souls reached with the Gospel.

For example, one chilly December morning Robert Mc Clements was visiting on the fringe of his district in a street where he had never been before. As he moved from house to house a very tidy-looking woman, whom he judged to be possibly in her late thirties, invited him to come in.

At a time when others were struggling to survive, Robert was surprised to find that the small living room was also extremely tidy and what little furniture there was appeared as though it had just been polished. One peculiar thing puzzled the missionary, though.

It was that there was no fire in the grate. By the look of it there hadn't been one for days, either, although the weather had been particularly frosty for nearly a week.

Robert sat with his overcoat and scarf wrapped tightly around him. His breath, when he spoke and later read the Bible and prayed, appeared in a vapour cloud before him. The room was icy cold.

As he rose to go he remarked, "Hasn't it been very cold recently?"

The neat little lady glanced towards the empty grate and when she blushed red with embarrassment if helped colour up her pale, drawn face.

Tears began to glint in her eyes.

"Oh, I'm sorry, sir, my house is so cold, but we have had to do without a fire for some time," she blurted out. "You see my husband has been out of work for a good while now and he is not eligible for unemployment benefit. I took a job to help earn some money but I have lost that too. We have no money whatsoever coming into the house now."

She perched herself on the arm of a chair, and sobbed softy as she continued, "I don't want the neighbours to know the way we have to live so I just try to appear as normal as possible. When Jim had a job we had plenty of money but he gambled a lot of it on the horses and now we have nothing."

Having paused to take a deep breath that ended like a long, sad sigh, she finished her pathetic little tale of woe with the words, "We are ruined. I just don't know what we are going to do!"

Robert Mc Clements left that home with a lump in his throat and a tear in his eye.

If the little tidy lady didn't know what she was going to do, he knew what *he* was going to do. It was what he felt His Lord would have done in the same set of circumstances.

He went along to a local grocer's shop and ordered a box of groceries to be sent to the house. Moving on another few streets he spoke to a coal merchant he knew and had two bags of coal delivered to the same address.

On the following Sunday evening Robert was pleased to welcome both husband and wife to the seven o'clock service in Derg Street Mission Hall. They began to attend regularly every Sunday and six months later the husband, Jim, was saved and his wife who had been a backslider was restored to the joy, which once she had known, in the Lord. Their lives were transformed and both husband and wife became members of a local Presbyterian Church, and diligent workers in Derg Street.

Telling someone of his conversion, two years after the event, Jim declared that he owed it to 'a Christian gentleman, a box of groceries and two bags of coal!'

The value of consistent, patient visitation was shown in the case of Jack, a man who Edwin Logan, the missionary attached to Bread Street Hall called in on regularly. When he was drunk Jack was the terror of the neighbourhood and when Edwin called at his door he was often given a rather frosty reception.

After at least a year of seeking to maintain the contact with him, Edwin found that Jack was beginning to mellow in his attitude.

Then late one Saturday afternoon, as he was walking down a street in his district, Edwin noticed that Jack was coming to meet him, looking thoroughly miserable.

"What's wrong with you today, Jack?" the missionary enquired.

"I'll tell you what's wrong with me," came the immediate and rather agitated response. I have been gambling and I have lost everything. I have even lost five pounds that I borrowed from another man. There is nothing left to live for and there is no point in anything any more. I am fed up and I'm thinking of going home to end it all."

Edwin stood on the street, reasoning gently with the downcast, disillusioned man for almost an hour. He told Jack of a Saviour who loved him, and would save him, if he would only come and trust Him.

The message of love and salvation seemed to fall on deaf ears, though, and eventually Jack said that he had go on.

"Just before you go, Jack, remember what I told you. God loves you, Christ died for you and He wants to save you," Edwin told him, trying to make the message as concise as possible. Then he repeated an invitation that he had extended to Jack, and which had been flatly refused, many times before.

"Why don't you come round to the meeting in Bread Street some Sunday night?"

A few weeks later Jack turned up at the Sunday evening service and started to attend occasionally.

One night Edwin had chosen as his text, 'What will you do with Jesus?' When he repeated the question as a challenge towards the close of the meeting Jack stood up, and with tears rolling down his cheeks cried out, "I will take Him!"

And he did.

There was an instant change in Jack. He became, at that moment, 'a new creation in Christ Jesus.' His home became the happy place that it should have been, and within two weeks, much to the surprise of his former cronies, he had paid off all his gambling debts.

It was interesting to observe, also, in those times of depression, how the light of the Gospel shone into lives and homes, bringing rays of hope in days of darkness. And the light that illuminated one life or home often affected others as well.

This was illustrated one Saturday night in the Mission Hall in Jersey Street.

The workers based in the Hall had met for their prayer meeting in preparation for a busy Sabbath day ahead in the service of the Lord when the door opened and a tall man entered. He appeared singularly unhappy.

"Who is in charge here?" he asked as he walked up the Hall.

John Kelly, the missionary in the district stepped forward. "I suppose you could say that I am," he replied, stretching out his hand to offer the visitor a hearty handshake. "You are very welcome. We are pleased to see you."

"Can you do anything for me?" the tall stranger went on to enquire, in a voice trembling with emotion. "I have played the fool and made a mess of my life. I want to be a man like my brother."

"And who is your brother? Do we know him?" John asked.

"You should know him," came the instant response. "Robert sings in your choir. He has been coming here for about three years."

John certainly remembered Robert. He had come into a meeting drunk, with a loaf of bread under his arm, and had listened attentively to the story of redeeming grace. At the end of the meeting he had trusted in Jesus as his Saviour.

"Oh yes," John continued with a smile. "Of course we know Robert. He comes here every week."

"Well can you to do for me what you have done for him?" his brother wanted to know. "He is so happy now."

"Would you like to take a seat there?" John asked the earnest enquirer before going on. "We can't do anything for you, really, but we can tell you of Someone who can, the Lord Jesus."

John then explained to him the wonderful truth of the Gospel and half-an-hour later he knelt down at a form, with John beside him and praying workers all around. They were all touched as he poured out his heart in simple language, confessing his sins and asking God to save him and change him.

In this case, the marvellous peace and joy that he had witnessed in his brother's home had been the catalyst that was used by God to lead him to repentance.

God was at work in the city in the midst of social unrest and extreme poverty.

In 1932 the Jersey Street Hall, which had been donated to the Mission by Mr. Thomas McBride, and in which Robert and his brother had come to know the Lord, had to be enlarged and additional seating provided.

There were so many people coming that the existing hall couldn't contain them all. Possibly the most notable aspect of the work, and one in which tremendous blessing was experienced in Jersey Street at that time was amongst the young.

The morning Sunday School had 10 teachers and 120 pupils, and in the afternoon there were 32 teachers and 500 pupils. Then on a Tuesday evening there was a Bible Class for young men and women with an average attendance of 130.

It would be difficult to overestimate the eternal interest on the spiritual investment that Thomas McBride made on behalf of the people of the Crumlin Road district of Belfast when he donated the Hall in Jersey Street to the City Mission.

When introducing one of his reports in the mid-thirties David Irwin J.P., remarked, 'In the world we see the triumph of science in dealing with waste matter, in making the ugly beautiful, the sterile fruitful and the useless thing valuable. In the work of the Belfast City Mission the triumphs of grace are also in evidence. We are seeing men and women rescued from the scrap heap and literally recreated. Where conditions appeared most hopeless, where effort seemed hardly worthwhile, we have seen victories won. Many who commenced the year in sin can now truly say, 'He brought me up out of an horrible pit and put a new song in my mouth."

He was right.

With the power and promises of God behind them the missionaries and their bands of loyal helpers were reaching out with the life-changing message of the Gospel to young and old, to the despondent and the destitute in homes, in halls and in the open air.

The Belfast City Mission was engaged in a massive reclamation initiative.

It was recycling people.

18

BLITZED!

Although the prospect of a Second World War was terrifying, especially to those who had lived through the terrors of the First, when Britain declared war on Germany in 1939, a period of full employment, and hence relative prosperity, followed for the people of Belfast.

The new four-engine Stirling, the first of the heavy bombers, was being developed in the Short & Harland aircraft factory which had been opened at Sydenham in 1936. Harland & Wolff began building warships round the clock, and James Mackie & Son rejigged to manufacture anti-aircraft shells. Soon after the outbreak of hostilities any able bodied adult in the city who hadn't joined the forces to fight on land, at sea or in the air, had a job in a factory of some sort, advancing the war effort.

Although there were to be privations caused by a shortage of imported food, yet it looked as if a measure of stability could return to the city. There was an added consolation for the people of Belfast in the knowledge that they were far enough away from Germany to be in no immediate danger of attack or invasion.

All that was to change, though.

When France fell to the advancing German armies in the summer of 1940, Belfast became within range of the enemy bombers operating from bases in that country. Its heavy manufacturing industries were producing warships, warplanes, and assorted weaponry, so it had to be considered a prime target.

It was.

On April 15, 1941, a total of two hundred Junkers, Heinkels and Dorniers unloaded a terrifying collection of blast bombs, time bombs and parachute bombs on the ill-prepared industrial city.

Devastation and death ensued.

The York Street Spinning Mill suffered what amounted to a direct hit. It collapsed in a pile of rubble which virtually obliterated two nearby streets. More that 30 people died in that one incident, and there were dozens more like it.

Then before the defences of Belfast could be strengthened, the bombers returned. Another wave of two hundred came back on May 4, targeting the shipbuilding yards and the aircraft factory. There were fewer civilian casualties in that second attack but the bombing had struck deep into the industrial heart of the city and so the setback to the war effort was more telling.

Nearly 900 people had been killed and more than 1,500 severely wounded on those two nights of bombing in the city. In addition, massive damage occurred to homes and business properties. About 2000 homes had been completely destroyed, 56,000 houses had been extensively damaged, and as a result of this widespread destruction 15,000 people had been rendered completely homeless.

Having wreaked such havoc on the city which it sought to serve, the air raids, and the threat of further repeat performances, had a profound impact on the work of the Mission in 1941.

Only one of their buildings, the Earl Street Mission Hall in the Docks area, was damaged in the attacks, but it was completely wrecked in the May raid. This left David Hamilton, who had just been appointed to the staff of the Belfast City Mission and assigned to Earl Street about six weeks earlier, without a base. He was transferred to Roden Street in a temporary capacity until another hall could be found for him in North Thomas Street. This permitted him to carry on the valuable work of visitation and consolation in the devastated York Street district.

The evacuation of the city into the country, which had begun rather half-heartedly in the previous year swung into operation on a massive scale after the April attack in 1941. This was for two reasons. It was considered prudent to move all the children out into safer rural areas and the homeless had to be re-housed. Since housing was totally unavailable in the city a contingency housing programme was put into effect across the province.

This mass exodus saw 50,000 people, mainly children and homeless families, relocated to provincial towns. This was the only possible course of action open to the authorities, but it created a challenge for all those involved in the Belfast City Mission.

The missionaries continued to work all the more vigorously amongst the people who remained, some of them in bereaved homes in battered houses, ministering to those who had lost loved ones, or had been injured in the bombing raids. This was a valuable work and they found themselves welcomed into homes where once they would have been refused entry. In some districts, however, the virtual total evacuation of some of the worst affected streets left them feeling frustrated.

They wanted to visit people, preach to people, or tell little children of the Saviour, but nearly everybody had gone!

Sabbath Schools became depleted, some of them having lost more than half of their pupils in a matter of weeks. Street visitation became difficult for in some districts whole streets had been wiped out. Fear of the wailing air-raid siren that would warn of the danger of another attack meant that people were loath to leave their homes to attend meetings.

Nearly every aspect of the work of the missionaries, especially those operating in city centre and dockland districts, had changed.

The sheer scale of what happened, and the problems it caused for the men on the ground, is expressed in the reports of two of them at the time.

On arriving home from an afternoon spent attempting to visit from door to door as once he had done, one man wrote in this journal,

'What is the Missionary to do who visits a street, and finds in it only one family, and who visits another street and finds in it only two families? Such has been my experience recently. Part of my district has been like a city of the dead; whole streets once full of people, for whose benefit we often held cottage and open-air meetings, are now denuded of their population, and are almost uninhabitable.'

A second missionary wrote,

'My district suffered severely during the recent air-raids. Whole families were wiped out, and great numbers of people injured and rendered homeless. In this terrible time I had wonderful opportunities of bringing comfort and encouragement to the people among whom I had worked for years. My own house was wrecked but I managed to get into a little home in the very heart of the district. This left me, in a real sense, 'sitting where they sat'.'

In situations such as those described, what *is* the Missionary to do?

Having prayed for guidance, they did at least three things.

Firstly, they went to where they knew that a number of people would be congregating. If people didn't feel disposed to going to mid-week services in the local Mission Hall, they had no choice but to rush along to the air-raid shelters when the sirens wailed across the city.

The missionaries moved from one packed shelter to another trying to cheer the frightened people by encouraging them to sing choruses. Many of the men were able to sing a solo and were pleased when some of the audience joined in with such well-known pieces as 'Rock of Ages', 'Jesus Lover of My soul' and 'Abide With Me'. Then after a short Gospel message they moved on to another shelter.

James Leetch was making his way out of a shelter one evening to press on towards the next when a woman in her seventies reached across and held him by the arm. "I haven't been in a church since I left Sunday School, sir" she said. "But that was really great."

A friend who had been there told him later that a number had wept after he left, having been challenged by the reality of the message in those uncertain times. Others said that it was 'the best shelter they had ever been in.'

In another district it became a part of the missionary, Samuel Haslett's usual procedure to move out into the streets, among the people, as soon as the siren sounded. He considered it an opportunity to reach the people at a time when he could be of most help to them.

One night as he led the crowd in the singing of hymns and choruses Samuel kept appealing to his audience to increase the volume to help drown out the drone of the bombers overhead. In a break between choruses he was cheered, challenged and just mildly amused to hear an elderly man remark to a companion, "We will be all right tonight for we have the missionary with us."

Although Samuel's trust was in God and he knew that nothing could happen to him outside of the will of his Heavenly Father, yet the whine and whistle of falling bombs sent a tingle of fear up his spine from time to time. It was good, nonetheless, that the old man found his presence so reassuring.

They didn't give up on the Sabbath School work, either. In one district, where the evacuation had seen a Sabbath School of over a hundred reduced to thirty the missionary and teachers began to pray for more pupils. Then, willing to put words into action they embarked upon a systematic visitation programme in the area, taking several surviving streets in the district every week, and going from door to door, inviting children along to the Hall. This proved to be a fruitful exercise for within two months their attendance was up to more than it had been before the evacuation, and whole families, who would not otherwise have been contacted, heard of the Saviour Who loves boys and girls, and calls them to Himself.

A third way in which the mission responded to the dramatic changes in the plight of the poor, amongst whom they worked, was that some of the missionaries followed the evacuees out into the country. It was a case of finding them, and assisting them where they were.

Missionaries, occasionally working in pairs, spent some time locating the evacuees in the homes which had been opened to them. Having found them in their unfamiliar environments they did what they could to help the city dwellers to adjust to the country way of life.

A pair, trying to contact evacuated families around Portadown found many of them disconsolate for they hadn't received their evacuation allowance, and had little or no money. The two men, on taking up their case with the billeting officer, found him most cooperative, and the displaced families soon received their payment.

The families were understandably pleased at this intervention on their behalf and when the missionaries arranged cottage meetings, one each night in different homes across a wide country area, many of them came.

These meetings were so popular amongst the evacuees that they begged the missionaries to continue. This they were only too happy to do, procuring the use of a centrally situated schoolroom.

Both the local people and their long term visitors up from the city turned out in force to these meetings and one of the missionaries, recalling that campaign at a later date said, "I never remember being in meetings where there was such a sense of God's presence."

This experience was repeated in other provincial towns where city missionaries kept in contact with the people from their district who had relocated by writing letters to them. They then followed them into their rural retreat for a short spell at least, organising meetings, and witnessing God's blessing amongst them. Very fruitful missions were conducted by city missionaries in Lurgan and Ballymena as well as in Portadown.

One of the effects of the blitz in Belfast was that it sent people fanning out across the countryside to experience a style of life that they could only have imagined beforehand. The persecution of the early Church in the Bible forced the Christians to spread out from Jerusalem taking their message of a risen conquering Saviour all across the country. So, too, when the city missionaries followed the evacuees from city streets into their rural setting, it presented them with opportunities to present the Gospel to communities they would not otherwise have reached.

The Belfast City Mission had come to the country in a most practical way, to the mutual benefit of both.

Further links were forged with country churches and in the years that followed a number of city missionaries would be invited to report on the ongoing work of the Mission, and conduct meetings, in them.

When presenting the report for 1941, Mr. David Irwin described it as having been 'one of the most trying and difficult in the history of the Mission, especially for the Missionaries and their workers'. He then went on to enumerate those difficulties. The missionaries had witnessed death and devastation at an unprecedented level, horrible injuries, homelessness, evacuation to the country, and the total destruction of a Mission Hall.

They had been 'blitzed', in every sense of the word.

Despite hardship piled upon hardship, however, the report went on to state that 'other avenues of approach were opened up.'

The amazing thing about it was that when these 'avenues opened up' the Mission committee, the city missionaries and their helpers were not overawed by the challenge.

They simply sought the help of God and launched out into the unknown, adapting to the circumstances, for the sake of the suffering souls of Belfast and the joy of serving their Lord and Master.

19

WHAT'S THE POINT?

The war rumbled on in Europe.

News of battles won lifted the spirits of the people of Britain but tidings of defeat and retreat caused gloom and despair. Such were the ups and downs of conflict.

Such too were the fluctuating successes and failures of the work of the Belfast City Mission.

On February 17, 1943, Dr. Henry Montgomery, who had been associated with the mission for almost sixty years, and who had been one of its honorary secretaries for forty-six, passed away. Dr. Montgomery had always advocated house-to-house visitation as the most effective means of evangelism and it was he who had inaugurated the Retired Missionaries Fund at the centenary meeting in 1927. Although he had been in failing health in his later years his advice and counsel had often been sought and was ever appreciated by the Mission committee.

In the work, and on the streets, it was often an uphill struggle for the missionaries. Visitation, though valuable, was a slow and often seemingly unrewarding exercise. Missionaries were occasionally tempted to think that certain individuals weren't worth bothering about, because of a life steeped in sin and vice and a total indifference towards God and the Gospel.

Andrew Orr came across a man like this when he was serving in the Ballynafeigh district of the city.

Frank had once been a prosperous businessman but he began to drink heavily and in the space of a few years his once promising and progressive concern, collapsed. The former owner, though out of business, carried on with his careless, drunken lifestyle until virtually penniless.

On hearing of Frank's situation Andrew called to visit him, only to be greeted with a torrent of abuse. When he told the man who was now down-and-out that he would return in a month's time, Andrew was advised, in language both profane and precise, that he would 'only be wasting his time.'

He did go back, though, a number of times, and seemed to make little headway whatsoever with Frank, who told him time and time again that he had 'no time for any sort of religion' and 'not to bother coming back.'

Andrew became disheartened. Could Frank have been spot on in the prediction that he had made at their first meeting? Was he just wasting his time?

Then Frank was admitted to hospital and Andrew visited him faithfully twice a week. He read a short scripture passage and prayed with the sick man on every visit, urging him to repent of his sin and give Christ a chance to change his life. Although not as abusive as formerly, Frank still refused to show any genuine interest in the message that Andrew was trying to present.

What is the point of all this? the missionary wondered to himself once or twice on his way home from the hospital in the tram. Frank is so hard-hearted I just don't seem to be getting though to him at all.

Struggling to overcome his reservations, Andrew continued to visit him when he was discharged from hospital. He also encouraged his Christian friends in the Kimberly Street Mission Hall to pray for Frank.

Apparently unprofitable months passed until one morning Andrew was somewhat bemused to be asked, completely out of the blue, to go and visit Frank. It was so out of character for the man who had once been so unresponsive to actually request a visit that Andrew responded as soon as possible.

When he arrived into the living-room of the little terrace house where Frank lived he found the man who had been so opposed to the Gospel sitting with a smile on his face.

"What has happened?" Andrew enquired, doubtful if the news could possibly be what he and his friends had been praying for.

"Three nights ago I wasn't too well so I went to bed early but couldn't sleep," Frank told him. "I couldn't understand it but the things you told me kept coming up over and over again in my head. I just couldn't get rid of them, no matter how hard I tried.

When I could hold out no longer I cried to God in the words of a hymn that were in a little book you gave me. I changed them a bit mind you. I said out loud,

Just as I am, without one plea,
But that Thy blood was shed for me,
And that Thou bidds't me come to Thee,
Oh Lamb of God – take me, for I come."

Andrew Orr was touched. It was almost three years since he had first called with this man, and he had often considered giving up on him.

A tear welled up in his eye as he asked, "And do you think he took you, Frank?"

"I do. He must have," came the reply, accompanied by a broad smile. "You see, Andrew, I haven't been the same man since."

Faithfulness, in spite of doubts, eventually led to Frank's salvation, but that was not the case with a man that Lewis Warke visited in the Grosvenor Road district.

As he was calling from house to house along a street one day the missionary found a door partly open and as there was no reply to his knock he pushed on it to see if there was anyone about.

Lewis discovered that the sole occupant of the house was an old man, who was lying on a bed in a downstairs room. There was very little furniture in the room. A large greyhound lay curled up at the foot of the bed.

When he began talking to the man in the bed Lewis found that he had difficulty speaking. He had suffered a stroke some time before and was unable to leave the house.

It was a sad story. The man had lived a selfish life and now that he had fallen ill it had become a lonely life as well. All his former companions had deserted him, and he told Lewis that the only friend he had left in the world was his greyhound.

The missionary spoke to the lonely old man about the Saviour and His love, and he lay and wept bitterly. When pressed to open his heart and let the One who had died for him on Calvary to come into his life, he stopped short.

"I will think it over," was all he would say.

And as far as Lewis could gather, he never did trust in Christ.

He died having a greyhound as his only friend, when he could have had a 'Friend that sticketh closer than a brother'

The work amongst the young could prove difficult at times, too.

Jim Bell had been appointed to Roden Street Mission Hall in 1941 to replace David Forbes who had left to take up a position as Scripture Reader with the Army. When he started into his autumn programme of Monday evening Children's meetings after the summer holidays in 1942, though, he found it hard going.

The kids around Roden Street were rough, tough and rowdy. And as their only source of amusement was playing around the streets the Monday night meeting in the Mission was a big night out for them. They saw it as somewhere to go to meet their friends, and 'have a bit of a laugh.'

Monday, September 13 was Jim's third night of the season and the Hall was packed. There seemed to be chattering children all over the place.

What impression could he ever make on such a crowd?

How could he ever persuade them to listen to anything he had to say?

The piano accordion was his only hope. Jim Bell had a big piano accordion and the children loved it when he played. As the music from the accordion filled the Hall the endless throb of persistent talking was transformed into an exaggerated enthusiasm of exuberant singing.

When the choruses were finished the missionary spoke to the capacity crowd of children about the love of God and how that Jesus was calling young people to trust in Him. It seemed pointless, for so many of his audience appeared so restless, but noticing that perhaps there were a few who were paying attention to what he had been saying he issued an invitation.

"If any of you boys or girls would like to become a Christian come back here to the Hall tomorrow night at seven o'clock and we can have a talk about it," he said.

It hardly seemed worthwhile.

Will anybody take my invitation seriously? he would no doubt wonder as he made his way home, exhausted.

What he wasn't to know then, however, was that the offer of the opportunity to return the following evening had presented Ernest McQuoid, a ten-year old who had been present at the meeting, with the chance he had been waiting for.

This young lad had often contemplated accepting Jesus into his heart. His godly mother had told him, and his younger brother John, frequently, about how she had come to know the Lord in Roden Street Mission Hall, many years before.

At school next day Ernest made up his mind. He was going to call at the Mission Hall at seven o'clock to see Mr. Bell. The time had come for him to give his life to Christ. His only worry was that there would be others there too. It would be great if he could be on his own, for then he could keep his salvation a secret until he chose to tell somebody.

That's not the way it worked out, though.

The McQuoid family lived in Roden Street and it was only a short walk from their door to the Hall. When Ernest arrived down into the building at the appointed time he discovered that another boy he knew, Jim McIlveen was there as well, and four girls.

There were six of them!

Jim Bell was thrilled.

He gathered the group of young people on two forms beside the coal stove and talked to them about Jesus and committing their lives to Him. Then they all knelt down on the rough wooden floor that seemed to bore its way up into the boys' bare knees, and Ernest McQuoid accepted Jesus into his heart. Before he left the Hall that evening he found that young Jim and the four girls had all done the same.

Jim Bell was overjoyed.

What's the point in beating my head against a brick wall with this crowd of rowdies? he had asked himself more than once. ·

Now he knew.

God had been working in the hearts and minds of six young children.

It was the same gracious God who had led the missionaries on the streets and in the Halls to carry on their labours for Him, in spite of their own personal doubts and misgivings, that had guided the Mission's longest serving General Secretary all the way through to his retirement in September, 1943, also.

Francis Mulligan had joined the Mission in 1898 and had been the missionary in charge of the McClure Street work until his appointment as successor to Mr. William Maxwell, in 1913.

The thirty years in which he had been secretary had been eventful in the history of the city of Belfast, and progressive, expansive, and blessed by God, often in a mighty manner, in the history of the Mission.

When Francis Mulligan had been appointed in 1913 there were twenty-three missionaries at work across the city. When he retired in 1943 there were twenty-nine.

When he had been appointed in 1913 the annual income of the Mission was less than £2,000. The annual income for 1943 was £9,952.

In his years as secretary many new halls had been erected and opened, and additional missionaries had been appointed, so that the agents of the Mission were reaching out with both material help and Christian teaching to every working-class area of the city.

Perhaps his greatest contribution to the advance of the Mission was neither in administration nor finance, however, but in warmth and wisdom. Francis Mulligan had been a respected confidante and friend, a true spiritual mentor to all the missionaries.

William Wylie, who had been his assistant for six years, was appointed as his successor. The new General Secretary had assumed the mantle of a great man, but he was someone with years of experience of the workings of the Mission in all its aspects, a deep love for God and a passion for evangelism.

He could do the job.

20

SHOULD WE NOT GIVE GOD THE GLORY?

With the expansion of the work of the Mission in the city, and with sufficient funding available, it was considered necessary to appoint an additional missionary to the existing staff in March 1944. Consequently Mr. Jackson Buick, a man in his twenties from Antrim, was interviewed, accepted, and posted to the mission district of Ligoniel.

The new missionary began a systematic visitation of the area, and prayed often-desperate prayers for some sort of break in the work, for it was discouraging at first. It seemed that no matter how hard he tried, or how much he prayed, he could never seem to muster any more than twenty or thirty middle-aged or elderly people to any meeting.

In January 1945, though, when the new missionary and the new General Secretary combined forces, things began to change. William Wylie was invited to conduct a gospel campaign in the Mission Hall for which Jackson Buick had assumed responsibility on the northern edge of the city.

That mission proved to be a time in which God answered the prayers of the missionary and his small but loyal band of helpers in that Hall in a most wonderful way. Crowds of people came along, right from the very first night. Then as Jackson and a number of the workers called at all the houses with invitations, and as news travelled around the area, even more people began to attend.

William Wylie had been saved years before under the preaching of W. P. Nicholson, 'at four o'clock on a Sunday afternoon in the town of Ballymena,' as he told his audiences often. His style of preaching resembled that of the forthright evangelist. It was straight, to the point, no-nonsense Gospel preaching, and the people of Ligoniel responded.

In the space of a three-week mission in the dead of winter more that fifty people passed through the enquiry rooms and a high percentage of them decided to give their lives to Christ. One of the most encouraging aspects of these conversions, too, was that many of those who came to the Lord for salvation were young people between the ages of fifteen and twenty-five. In calling young men like Jim Pedlow and many others to Himself, God had, in His wisdom, laid the foundation for a productive testimony in the Gospel in Ligoniel.

This was to be very practically demonstrated a few months later.

When the Second World War eventually ended in May 1945 Belfast became a city swallowed up in celebration. The fear of another blitz and the inconvenience of the prolonged 'black-out' were gone.

On the evening of VE Day the floodlights around the City Hall and the Albert Memorial were switched on again for the first time in six years. As two of the city's best-known landmarks were illuminated against the darkening evening sky resounding cheers rang from the throats of the thousands of revellers thronging the streets.

As the celebrations for the Ligoniel district were being planned for that evening, and as the final collections were being made for the bonfires, some of which had already been built in anticipation of the end of the war, Jackson Buick met Mrs.Halfpenny on the street. Although she had never attended any of the meetings in the Mission Hall, 'Mrs. Hapeny' as the locals knew her, was a very religious woman and she had a heart-searching question for the missionary.

"Do you not think we should be giving God at least some of the glory for all of this, son?" she wanted to know.

"I think we should. You're right," Jackson was quick to agree with her sentiments. "In fact I think we should be giving Him not some, but all of the glory."

As he left her to go on his way, the young man was challenged. How, he wondered, could he best lead the people in his Hall in giving God the glory for the victory in battle?

All the churches across the province had already begun to contemplate the arrangements for their own particular Praise and Thanksgiving Services and some of missionaries in the Belfast City Mission Halls had begun to do likewise.

Jackson Buick had an idea. He sent word to as many as he could contact, and they in turn told others, that they were to meet at the Hall on the evening of VE Day.

When a large number of enthusiastic Christians turned up, Jackson told them of the plan he had, no doubt planted in his mind by God, to give Him the glory and use the opportunity to contact others for Him as well. With so many receptive people out on the streets he proposed that they should go round all the bonfires in the district singing God's praise and presenting the Gospel. They might never be given the chance to hold such massive open-airs again!

It worked!

After a brief period of prayer, the missionary set out, accompanied by a large group, including many of the young people who had come to faith in Christ in the January meetings. They were determined to go around as many of the bonfires as they could, reaching as many people as possible, with news of the greatest peace deal ever accomplished on behalf of mankind, God's salvation.

When they arrived at the first bonfire on their route the young people formed themselves into a tight circle, two and three deep, and began to sing well-known hymns. Then Jackson preached.

When they were finished there, they moved off towards bonfire number two to repeat the performance. As the itinerant team moved through the streets, singing as they went, they were pleasantly surprised that others seemed to be joining them.

On arriving at their second bonfire the group had grown considerably, and they sang again, and the missionary preached once more, as before.

The size of the crowd, when the still expanding group arrived at the third of the bonfires they had planned to visit, proved a problem. There were so many people milling about that the group found it difficult to find a suitable place to begin their open air.

The missionary had Zacchaeus–type stature problems. Jackson Buick was not the tallest man that the Belfast City Mission had ever appointed, and as he looked at the heaving mass of enraptured people all around he wondered how he could ever make himself heard.

The young men in his party soon solved the problem for him, though.

There weren't many sycamore trees around that particular site, but there was an old air-raid shelter, and a band of strong lads from the group lifted him on to the roof of it. Then the enlarged crowd of singers formed themselves into an impromptu choir that encircled the by-then thankfully obsolete building. When they began to sing the well-known words of the twenty-third Psalm, many curious bystanders gravitated towards the shelter.

Following a hearty rendering of a few more familiar hymns, Jackson preached the Good news of everlasting peace and freedom from the roof of a building, which held for many very stark memories of days of war and oppression. Hundreds stopped to listen.

When the singing, preaching, praising group reached the last of the four bonfires just after one o'clock in the morning, the party had swollen to almost four hundred! And that was just the moving, marching group!

There was another receptive crowd waiting to join in the singing and listen to the message from the missionary, around the dying remains of the final bonfire.

When Jackson Buick arrived home daylight was beginning to streak its way back across the May sky. His voice had almost gone, his face was smeared with smuts from the fires, but he was happy.

God had been given the glory, and souls had heard of His salvation.

News of the open-air meeting on VE Day soon spread to the central office in Fisherwick Place and Mr. F.J. Holland, the President, made a reference to it when speaking to some of the Mission staff later in the week.

Although the innovative endeavours of the energetic missionary in Ligoniel brought high praise from some, it struck a sense of fear and foreboding into at least one other.

Young Jim Davidson had just taken up, on May 1, his first appointment with the Mission as agent in Cuba Street, thus replacing Mr. Matthew Campbell who had retired. He had only been in post about a fortnight when he heard the President tell, with obvious pleasure, of the round the bonfires preaching parade.

And it scared him!

If that's what you have to do as a Belfast City missionary I doubt I'm in the wrong job, he thought to himself. I could never do that kind of thing!

Jim had a different quality, though. It was that of a quiet, winsome, godly disposition and he asked the friends in Cuba Street to help him mark VE Day in his own unassuming way.

"We are going to have a Special Thanksgiving Service next Sunday evening," he announced one week. "I would like everyone in the Hall here to try and bring at least one of their neighbours into it. I will be doing my best during the week to contact as many people as possible myself. We want to thank God for the national victory He has given us in the War and tell others of the personal victory He can still give us in Christ."

Although he had only been their missionary for a short time Jim had endeared himself to the workers in Cuba Street, and knowing that he would keep his word and invite as many as he could, many of them also brought neighbours along. Some of the people who came to the Special Thanksgiving service that Sunday evening had never been in the Mission Hall before.

One such person was Bobby Watt.

Bobby was a plater in the shipyard and a rough character. He was more often drunk than sober, especially at the weekends and all the children in his street were afraid of him. Two single sisters, however, who lived opposite him, invited him along to the special service and he promised them, in one of his more coherent, and possibly weaker moments that he would go.

When the two sisters called across at Bobby's house on the evening of the meeting they discovered, not surprisingly, that he was under the influence of alcohol. He insisted on going with them, though, and they walked him round to the Hall in Cuba Street. The two ladies then set themselves at either side of their neighbour and prayed silently that he wouldn't disturb the meeting.

Their prayers were answered. Although still drunk Bobby didn't make a nuisance of himself, and when the service was over he said to his two slightly concerned custodians, "I would like to talk to that man."

When most of the others had left the Hall one of the ladies said to Jim, "The man we brought with us says he would like to speak to you."

Jim went up to where 'the man' was, having risen to try and walk about restlessly.

He introduced himself and then enquired if he could be of help.

"Yes, you can," came the immediate, mumbled reply. "I'm Bobby Watt, and I'm drunk, but I want to get saved. What can you do for me?"

"I can point you to the Lord Jesus, and He can do marvellous things for you," Jim told him. "Come on into this wee room at the back and we will have a chat."

When Bobby had made his way slowly into the enquiry room the new missionary on the district sat down beside him and told him of the consequences of sin, the love of God for sinners and the sacrifice of Christ to put away sin. He then explained to Bobby that if he trusted in the Lord Jesus, He would forgive his sin, and make a new man out of him.

An hour or so later Jim knelt alongside Bobby as the man who had been the drunken character of the area opened his heart to the Lord Jesus.

As he walked home much later that evening, Jim poured out his heart in thanksgiving to God. The verse that kept running through his mind was a part of what Paul wrote to some Christians in Corinth nearly two thousand years before, and which had been on so many lips on so many services over the VE Day celebration.

It was, "But thanks be to God, which giveth us the victory through our Lord Jesus Christ'.

Jim hadn't felt himself suited to preaching in large, successive open air meetings but he had seen, within the first month of his ministry with the Mission a most remarkable conversion. And Bobby Watt was later to become a tremendous testimony in the area and a tireless worker in the Cuba Street Hall.

Both Jackson Buick and Jim Davidson had reinforced for them, in May 1945, as young men setting out in Christian service, that the battle, and the victory, were, and could only be, God's.

They were prepared, also, to give Him all the glory.

21

THE WAR IS OVER,
BUT THE WORK GOES ON

The end of the War brought big changes for the people of Belfast.

A crash programme of house building was the most pressing priority. The situation had become desperate in some districts. Multiple families were living in single houses. New dwellings were needed urgently to replace those which had been obliterated in the blitz or condemned as being unfit for human habitation.

The Housing Trust was set up and began building its first estates at Cregagh, Finaghy and Andersonstown. Prefabricated bungalows were hastily erected at Beechmount, Shore Crescent, Annadale Embankment and a number of other sites across the city.

Gradually families who had been displaced by the privations of war were re-housed and new communities were established.

The shift in population occasioned by extensive re-housing projects was one of the two issues that the Belfast City Mission had to address with the return of a period of relative peace to the city, the country and the world. The other was to cultivate the growing interest in the Mission within Presbyterian Churches in rural districts. This awareness was awakened, at least in some cases, by the number of evacuees, followed by missionaries who worked for brief periods amongst them, relocated from the city to the country in the early 1940's.

In the second half of 1945 many requests came into the Mission office inviting the committee to send a missionary to conduct special meetings in connection with the Simultaneous Victory Mission in Presbyterian churches across the province. Much blessing was experienced and many were brought into a saving relationship with Christ in campaigns in Ahorey, Clare and Richill (Co. Armagh) Castlecaulfield and Benburb (Co. Tyrone) Crossgar, Drumgooland and Kilkinamurry (Co. Down) and Dundrod and Loanends (Co. Antrim). Other fruitful missions were held in some of the larger provincial towns, most notably in Greenwell Street, Newtownards; High Kirk, Ballymena; and Sloan Street, Lisburn.

In an attempt to maximise the widening interest in the Mission and to help extend both its prayer and financial basis for the furtherance of the work and to give the praise and glory to God for His goodness, the directors decided to appoint a missionary with specific responsibilities for such matters.

The person they chose for this newly created post was David Hamilton, a man with his roots in the country. David had come into the city to work in the mission in 1941, from his home on a farm outside Kells, County Antrim. He was released from his work in the York Street area on November 1, 1945, to 'devote his full time to deputation work, conducting special missions in town and country and the opening of new Auxiliaries'.

David's natural ability as an administrator and his God-given gift for evangelism made him a most suitable person to fill the post, but the people of the district where he had built up valuable contacts for God were sad to see him go.

Two such young men were Cecil Robinson and Jim Charters.

Cecil was a teenager when David Hamilton called at his house in 1942 to speak to his mother who had been ill. On his way out of the house he invited the lad to come along to the Bible Study he had started for boys and young men in the upstairs room in North Thomas Street. The use of this accommodation had been granted to the Mission by St. Enoch's Presbyterian Church following the bombing of the Earl Street Hall in the blitz of 1941.

Although he had always lived what he considered an ordinary, clean sort of a life, when Cecil began attending David Hamilton's Bible Study he realised that he was not yet ready to meet God. He needed to be saved. The desire to come to Jesus grew within him and he was glad when David asked one evening, just as he was about to go down the stairs to go home, "Well, Cecil, what about you? When are you going to come to the Lord?"

"I have been thinking about that, Mr. Hamilton," the teenager replied, after only a brief hesitation. "I would like to come to Him tonight."

"Would you like to wait behind with me and we can talk about it?" the missionary enquired, sensing Cecil's concern.

The lad was happy to have someone speak to him about the Lord Jesus and after some conversation David and he knelt down beside the little gas fire and Cecil gave his life to the Lord. The sense of peace and joy that crept over his soul received a gentle jolt when he reached home, though.

"Those conversion experiences never last any longer than a month or six weeks," his parents told him. "You'll get over it."

That was sixty years ago, and Cecil hasn't 'got over it' yet!

David Hamilton then began to teach Cecil, Jack Devenney and a number of other new believers about the importance of Bible reading, prayer, and living a consistent Christian life. The missionary became their valued spiritual guide.

Jim Charters had a different experience.

He had become a Christian before he ever began attending the meetings up the stairs in North Thomas Street, but had gradually lapsed into a careless, backslidden condition.

When he started to attend the Mission meetings David Hamilton must have reckoned that the nineteen year old had spiritual potential for he asked Jim to teach a Sunday School class.

Not having the courage to confess his true condition Jim began to teach a group of young boys but he found it difficult. Reading the Bible in order to prepare his lessons became a challenging chore.

He couldn't escape the voice in his head, which kept saying, "You hypocrite. You hypocrite!"

The situation came to a head one evening at a Sunday School teachers' meeting. David had invited all the teachers to engage in chain prayer, praying one by one for their classes and for the work of the Sunday School.

A cold sweat began to break over Jim Charters. What was he going to do? How could he pray for anybody?

When it came his turn he stood up and opened his mouth, but no words came.

He just stood there opening and closing his mouth spasmodically, like a fish.

After ten silent seconds he sat down.

At the end of the meeting he apologised to David for his inability to pray, confessing that although he was a Christian he was really far away from the Lord in his heart.

David understood, and when the others had gone he read some Bible passages with the worried Sunday school teacher. He then encouraged him to try praying again, acknowledging and repenting of his waywardness to the Lord, for, he assured Jim, God is always willing to pardon His erring children and restore to them the joy that they once had known.

This time it worked.

Jim opened his mouth to pray and the words actually came.

The missionary's prediction proved to be true also, for when Jim confessed his wandering ways before the Lord, and begged forgiveness, the young man had the peace and satisfaction of God's salvation returned to him in abundant measure.

There were a number of changes in the mission staff following the war, in addition to the appointment of David Hamilton as evangelist and Auxiliary co-ordinator.

Mr. James Irvine retired and Mr. John Girvan, a young man from Killinchy, County Down, was appointed to the Mission Hall work he had left on Donegall Road. The idea of emigration appealed to some and four missionaries left to take up positions with the Canadian Home Mission. John Luke, William Ernest Harper, Robert Smith and William Wilson were appointed to fill the vacancies.

In the midst of the change taking place all around there were times when those involved in the Mission stopped to reflect, and mark milestones in the goodness of God.

The Jubilee meeting in the Boyd Endowment School on the Ravenhill Road was just such an occasion.

'The Boyd', as it was known in the district, was one of three buildings funded from a bequest by one Hugh Henry Boyd, and erected in different city locations. The first of these was opened in Mayo Street in 1889, the second at the lower end of the Ravenhill Road in 1897 and the third in Roden Street in 1903. These buildings were designed with a dual purpose, operating as schools during the day from Monday to Friday and as 'preaching houses' on Sundays and for as many evenings as they were required during the week.

On December 12, 1948, 'The Boyd' was packed with friends of the Belfast City Mission to mark fifty years of consistent work for God in that area and in that building. Some of those attending that evening had actually been present at the official opening on July 31, 1897!

A variety of speakers paid tribute to the value of the work that had been accomplished for God in the advancement of His kingdom in the Hall under the supervision of Mr. Samuel Brown. This local businessman had commenced a Sunday School in 'The Boyd' as an outreach of the Belfast City Mission.

When the children of the district began to come regularly, and bring others with them, Mr. Brown soon recognised that he needed help. He applied to the Mission for the services of a full-time missionary, promising to contribute fifty pounds per annum towards his salary.

The directors of the Mission readily accepted his offer and Mr. William Smith was appointed and became City missionary to the district for a number of years.

Two serving missionaries, one who had begun his career with the Belfast City Mission in 'The Boyd', Mr. William Lynas, and the man who was currently in charge of the work there at that time, Mr. William Anderson, also took part in the proceedings on that 'jubilee' evening.

There were many smiles and knowing nods of the head when William Lynas recounted how he arrived, as a mere twenty-two year old, to preach his 'trial sermon' in 'The Boyd' in June 1912.

"I can see a number here tonight who were here on the first night I ever stood on this platform," he began," and I want to tell you this, you are now almost thirty seven years older. I did not know Mr. Brown until that night but Mr. Smith, in whose footsteps I was very conscious that I would be expected to follow, was there. He led the meeting for me but he seemed to get through all the introductions very quickly and had me standing up here at twenty past eight."

The speaker paused a moment to make eye-contact with some of the local stalwarts before continuing with a twinkle in his eye, "And he left me too much time! I preached on for as long as I could, but I still had to let the people out fifteen minutes early.

As I stepped down from the platform, I thought that I had let myself down, and that the City Mission wouldn't want a man who couldn't preach out the time. When I was speaking to some of the people from the Hall afterwards, though, a man whom I later discovered to be Mr. Brown came across to me and remarked, "At least you had the sense to stop when you were finished. That is a point in your favour."

It must have been, too, for in the middle of the week I received a letter from the City Mission office, giving me a starting date! I spent seven happy years here before moving on to McClure Street where it is still my privilege to serve the Lord and the people of that district."

William Anderson, on welcoming all the friends of the Mission in the Boyd Endowment Hall told the audience that when he had joined the City Mission as a twenty-one year old he thought he 'knew it all'. A few years under the supervision of Mr. Brown, however, showed him that there was much he had to learn about dealing with people in the service of the Lord.

"One thing he kept telling me," Mr. Anderson went on, " when he was booking another preaching engagement for me somewhere, was that I should always count it a privilege and an honour to preach the Gospel. He kept me on the right lines but I have to confess that I was glad of him, not only for his advice and encouragement, but also for another, less noble, reason."

It was his turn to survey the audience, many of whom would know who he was talking about, before continuing, "When I ran up against Mrs. So-and-so who complained that the Hall was too hot...or too cold, or that the meetings were too long...or too short, I just blamed it on Mr. Brown!"

Before resuming his seat William Anderson summed up the work of the Mission in 'The Boyd' in a most telling way.

He began by reading a letter from a Mr. Cleland from Scotland. In the course of the letter the correspondent claimed to have been one of the first converts at the Mission on Ravenhill Road.

William then went on to tell his audience, "I was visiting in the City Hospital last week, but when I arrived at a certain ward I found that the lady I had called to see had been discharged. The woman in the next bed spoke to me and said, "Mr. Anderson, she was sorry to miss you, but left a message with me to tell you that she has decided for Jesus Christ." The woman hesitated a minute and then said to me, "And by the way, I have trusted Him too."

The man who had, up until that date, worked tirelessly in the Boyd for twenty years allowed his eyes to scan down across the crowded congregation before concluding, "Fifty years ago people were deciding for Christ in this district. And they are still deciding."

How true! How thrilling!

And that was only in one Hall out of twenty-nine.

There were dedicated missionaries in twenty-eight others who would have similar tales to tell!

22

WHAT WILL I DO WITH JESUS?

It was in late January 1947 that Robert Lilley was bringing the cows in for milking one Saturday morning, at the Sheddings, on the road between Ballymena and Carnlough in County Antrim. As he looked across to the main road from the door of the byre he saw Mr. David Hamilton walking along towards the bus stop, probably to catch a bus back to Belfast.

David Hamilton had almost completed a two-week mission in a church nearby and a number of the local Christians, having attended regularly, had been impressed by both the spiritual depth and genuine sincerity of the Belfast City Mission evangelist.

Having tied up the cows, Robert Lilley walked down to the bus stop. When he had introduced himself as having 'been at the meetings in Killyharn and Buckna a number of nights' he asked, "Would you consider holding a mission in Carnalbanagh Presbyterian Church across the country from here, Mr. Hamilton, if it could be arranged?"

"Yes, I'm sure I would," David Hamilton replied to the sudden, solo request. "I would have to pray about it though, and it would have to be approved by the minister and session of the church."

A year passed in which approval for a campaign in Carnalbanagh was procured and David Hamilton began his mission in the

Presbyterian Church in the County Antrim village on Sunday, April 4, 1948.

It was spring in the country and sowing and planting time. Farmers were busy in the fields and some were sceptical of the idea of holding a mission in such a busy period.

"Nobody will come," the said.

How wrong they were proved to be!

David Hamilton had been reared on a farm and he understood the scene as well as anybody. "I want you to come just as you are," he told his congregations, right from the very first night. "You don't need to worry about dressing up fancy. I won't mind if you come in straight out of the fields. Just come!"

And come they did, in their hundreds.

During the first week the news of the meetings in Carnalbanagh Presbyterian Church caused a buzz in the district. People who had never been in the church in their lives came along to hear David Hamilton preach. He was a man sent from God for that community at that time.

The gentle buzz of interest that had stirred in the first week became an electrifying hum in the second. Every evening the narrow roads around the village, nestled among the softly rolling hills of the Antrim Plateau, were thronged with people walking three or four abreast, or cycling, to the mission.

Then in the middle of the second week people began to remain behind after the services to walk unashamedly into the enquiry room, seeking salvation.

What was happening in Carnalbanagh soon became 'the talk of the countryside'. God had created a longing for the peace and joy that is only to be found through faith in Him, in the hearts and minds of this hard-working self-righteous country community. New words and phrases such as 'salvation', 'redemption', being 'born again' and having 'new life in Christ' seemed to be on everybody's lips. Some had never heard of such a thing before and thought that this man David Hamilton had come to set up some sort of a new sect in the district.

This was not the missionary's intention at all, as everyone who knew him was well aware. His sole aim was to see souls come to the

Saviour, and he saw it achieved in a remarkable way in Carnalbanagh.

They continued to come, both to the mission, and to the Lord, and the news continued to spread. Names began to be mentioned. "Did you hear about Pat...or Elsie...or Johnny...they have got converted?" people asked each other, bemused.

Towards the end of the second week the tea breaks and lunch breaks in the local creamery were extended in the unprecedented circumstances. This was not because the employees didn't want to work. It was merely that they had become so preoccupied with discussing 'the new birth' and what some saw as 'this apparently compelling urge to run to religious meetings' that time, and work, became irrelevant.

On Friday night, April 16, David Hamilton held his congregation spellbound as he gave an account to the work that was so dear to his heart, that of the Belfast City Mission. He told of what life was like in the city when the work began, and then brought his report up to date by describing the dedication service, held on August 23, 1947, of the new Earl Street Hall, which the War Damage Commission had granted permission to have rebuilt on the original site. David also mentioned Cecil Robinson, a young man who had come to know the Lord, and had become a valued teacher in the Sabbath School run by workers from Earl Street, but accommodated in the more spacious surroundings of Sinclair Seamen's Church Hall.

The people of Carnalbanagh, many of whom had only been Christians for a matter of days, were thrilled to hear of this work, which had been carried on amongst the poor of Belfast for more than one hundred and twenty years, and decided to establish an auxiliary group to assist in the work.

Sunday, April 18 was to be the final night of the campaign and an hour before the evening service was due to begin one of the church elders arrived at the home where the missionary was lodging, and making final preparations for the service.

He had an unusual request to make.

"Mr. Hamilton, can you come soon and start the service?" he asked. "For the church is packed, the people are waiting, and we aren't going to be able to get any more in anyway!"

The missionary was taken to the church as soon as possible and the service began. Men, women, boys and girls had been crammed into every available space.

There was an air of expectancy about the place.

David Hamilton chose as his text for the evening the words of Jesus' summary of the spiritual condition of the enquiring scribe as recorded by Mark in his Gospel, 'Thou art not very far from the kingdom of God.'

A rapt, reverent, holy hush descended on the gathering as David spoke. Then as he was about to finish he appealed for all those whom he knew to be 'not very far from the kingdom of God' to step into it through faith in Christ, and many responded. The enquiry room was crowded with concerned, seeking souls after the service and thirteen people accepted Jesus into their hearts. One of these was a young man called Nat Rea, who was later to become a close friend of the missionary, and prayer supporter both of David and the work of the Belfast City Mission.

Throughout the 1950's David, as evangelist and ambassador of the Mission, endeavoured to branch out into different rural areas of the province, conducting special Gospel campaigns, and highlighting the needs of the Mission.

In April 1951 he returned to his home district, holding meetings in Cromkill School, close to where he had been brought up. He was pleased to see a number of his former neighbours come to faith in Christ at that time.

Another mission in which something of a mini-revival, along the lines of what happened in Carnalbanagh, was witnessed, was held in Armaghbrague Presbyterian Church, County Armagh, for three weeks in November 1953.

It was in the middle week of that series of meetings before anyone came to the Lord, but by the third week it appeared that the 'windows of heaven' had been thrown open wide in blessing. By the end of that November mission, more than forty people, and many of them teenagers, had come to Christ for salvation. On the last Friday night David preached from Pilate's despairing question, 'What shall I do then with Jesus, who is called Christ?' and fifteen people were counselled, seeking salvation.

Sunday night, 22 nd, was the final night and four hundred people jammed into the small country church, and a number decided for Christ.

There were a number of other rural churches in which David Hamilton conducted campaigns which he considered blessed by God. These included Closkelt in County Down in 1952, First Garvagh in 1954, Toberkeigh near the north coast in 1955, and Killymurris outside Ballymena late in 1959. In each of these outreaches David was careful to devote an evening to acquainting his audiences with the practical work and spiritual witness carried on by the Belfast City Mission. In such meetings he would include anecdotes from the long history of the Mission, incidents from his own experience and first hand news of the latest developments. He would then seek to set up an auxiliary group to support the Mission in that district. David also undertook single night deputation work, visiting churches all over the province, introducing congregations to, or updating them on, the vision of the Belfast City Mission.

In this way David Hamilton fanned into flame sparks of interest that had already floated down into remote rural districts, and lit fires of enthusiasm in sympathetic churches in provincial towns and along hawthorn-hedged country roads. This, in turn, was to lead to the inauguration of a network of auxiliary groups across the province, each offering prayer and financial support to the Mission.

Although he spent much time travelling across the country in the little Ford Anglia car that Nat Rea and a number of other Christian businessmen arranged to have purchased for him, David was always conscious, as an evangelist, that he had a duty also to the Halls of the Mission scattered across Belfast.

How, he no doubt reasoned to himself, can I speak intelligently of the work that is being carried on for God in the name of the Mission in the city, if I fail to keep in contact with the missionaries on the ground, or am never in any of the Halls?

David made a point, therefore, of keeping himself abreast of events within the Mission and accepting invitations to conduct gospel campaigns in the various Halls, visiting at least one every year.

From late February through into early March 1951 he preached for three weeks in Mayo street. In early October of that same year he preached for three weeks in Beechpark, and in November he spent a further three weeks in Kimberley Street.

In clear, early autumn weather in October 1952 the evangelist conducted a particularly fruitful mission in Mountcollyer Hall. Many local people attended and on the Sunday nights the Hall was filled to capacity with more that two hundred people packed in. More than twenty people came to faith in Christ during that three-week campaign and more than half of them were under twenty years of age.

David also spoke at missions in Jersey Street in March 1954, in Donegall Road in January 1955 and in Bellevue Street in October 1956.

In some of his Gospel missions across the city the blessing of God was experienced in a significant and visible manner. In others the evangelist couldn't help feeling a little discouraged. It wasn't always easy, but David Hamilton constantly maintained that it would only be in eternity that the ultimate outcome of any outreach for God could be adequately assessed.

1955 was a year of concerted evangelism in Belfast.

The Harringay Crusade, conducted by Dr. Billy Graham in London the previous year, and the 'Tell Scotland' Crusade in Glasgow, had focussed the minds of many across Britain on spiritual matters. Radio, television, and relayed services into public buildings and church halls, brought the truth of the Gospel, as it was being preached by Dr. Graham 'across the water', into homes and hearts still unfamiliar with its message.

The Jack Schuler Crusade in the King's Hall, at Balmoral on the outskirts of Belfast, in June-July '55, turned out to be a time when many, whose interest had been aroused, found the peace and satisfaction they had been seeking, through faith in Christ. The Belfast City Mission became very involved in the organisation of that Crusade, with many of the missionaries and mission workers acting as advisors, counsellors and stewards. Bus loads were brought from the different mission districts to the King's Hall each night and missionaries who had visited patiently up and down rows upon rows of houses in neat little streets had the pleasure of seeing some whom they had contacted committing their lives to the Lord.

In the autumn of the year the Presbyterian Church organised the '1955 Mission' when a simultaneous province-wide campaign was held in an effort to reach non-churchgoers with the Gospel. City missionaries were released from the work in their own districts to conduct special meetings in churches in the towns and country districts outside Belfast. In addition to David Hamilton, who as the mission's evangelist conducted a number of missions, Thomas Robinson was sent to Armagh Road, Portadown, David Magill to Richill, and Thomas Forbes to The Mall, Armagh, all in 'the orchard county.' William Anderson conducted a mission in Conlig, County Down and Jackson Buick was invited to speak in Dundrod, County Antrim.

The services of the city missionaries, preaching in the country, were very much appreciated by the various congregations, and in a number of cases men and women were won for Christ and many new names were added to the church registers.

The organising committee of the City Mission would always be first to acknowledge that their most valuable and lasting work for God amongst the poor people living in the streets of Belfast was done in visiting them in their homes. They also appreciated the value of short, focussed, Gospel campaigns, and with the approach of 1959, the centenary of 'The Year of Grace', an intensive programme of evangelism was planned, combining both these essential elements of outreach, and entitled, '1959, The Year of Opportunity.'

As part of this programme the city was divided into eight centres and the missionaries based in each centre combined in a schedule of methodical door-to-door visitation, ensuring that every house in each district was reached with the Gospel message. Then on Sunday, April 5, 1959, a special evangelistic Mission began in every Hall across the city, conducted by members of the Mission staff. David Hamilton preached for three weeks in the Ravenhill Road Hall, and other missionaries moved across to different districts to present the good news of salvation.

With the amount of planning that had gone into those events in 'The Year of Opportunity', the volume of prayer that had ascended to heaven on their behalf, and the degree of expectation that had built up in anticipation of another 'Year of Grace', the eventual spiritual outcome was rather disappointing.

Some, but relatively very few in proportion to the numbers actually contacted, decided for Christ.

The mission report for the year summarised the reaction of those involved very succinctly. It stated,

'Nineteen hundred and fifty-nine was a year that held out for us great expectations of another world-wide spiritual awakening, as in 1859, but it has come and gone and, alas, the spiritual fervour has deteriorated to a greater extent than ever before.

God is not in all their thoughts.'

When David Hamilton had used the words of Pilate, 'What shall I do then with Jesus?' as a challenge when preaching in Armaghbrague Presbyterian Church, fifteen people responded by accepting Him as their Saviour. There had been at least two hundred and fifty people present that night, however, so it is no doubt safe to assume that many more than fifteen left rejecting Him.

When Pilate had asked the question of the Jewish nation, almost two thousand years before, their vociferous, vehement response had been, 'Away with him! Crucify Him! We don't want this man to reign over us!'

And that still seemed to be the attitude of the vast majority of the people of Belfast.

Although there were occasional moments of blissful rest and refreshing along the way, the road stretching ahead of the Belfast City Mission remained, as it had always been, an uphill climb.

23

TO *EVERY* CREATURE?

In the late 50's and early 60's two changes took place in the leadership of the Belfast City Mission. Two men who had served the Mission faithfully for many years were both forced to retire owing to ill health.

William Wylie had been an efficient administrator and financial agent, but he never lost his ardour as an evangelist. When Rev. W.P. Nicholson revisited Ulster a programme of meetings was arranged which he was physically unable to complete in its entirety. On realising that his failing health was going to preclude him from fulfilling all his engagements the aged evangelist called up the only understudy in Ulster he would trust to take his place, his friend William Wylie. The general secretary of The Mission covered for Rev. Nicholson on a number of occasions but the strain was to prove almost too much for him also.

In the summer of 1959 Mr. Wylie was advised by his doctors to reduce his workload for the sake of his health and so he tendered his resignation.

In a tribute to his work, upon the announcement of his enforced resignation, the committee recorded in its report for 1959,

'During his service with Belfast City Mission Mr.

Wylie has devoted himself wholeheartedly to the furtherance of its work in every department. As an earnest evangelist, he has seen much blessing, not merely in the city but also throughout Ulster, where souls have been won and many friends and supporters have been recruited for his Master's work.

In matters of finance and administration his zeal and ability have been outstanding. He has been unsparing of himself and the results are reflected in the success of our Mission, and the position and standing it holds in the religious life of the community.'

His diligence as financial secretary was reflected in the figures available at the end of the year. When William Wylie had been appointed in 1945 the annual income of the Mission was £9,993 and when he retired in 1960 it was £20, 602. The annual income to the Mission had more than doubled in his fifteen years of office. A breakdown of that figure for 1960 would reveal that well over half of it, indeed in excess of £14,000, was classified as having been received as 'Subscriptions and Donations'.

At least some of that amount would have been raised by the tireless efforts of the man who had been Mr. Wylie's assistant for a number of years, and who the directors appointed as his successor in April,1960. On requesting for him the prayers and cooperation of all the staff and friends of the mission they described the incoming General Secretary as 'a young man of ability and enterprise who has been used by God in his evangelistic services both in the city and throughout the province.'

His name was David Hamilton.

Mr. F.J Holland, who had been one of the Mission's longest serving Presidents, having occupied the position with honour for almost twenty-five years, was forced to resign, also because of ill health, in 1961. He had served the Mission for more than forty years and superintendents, missionaries and workers of all kinds had always appreciated his advice and support. Mr. T.H. Jemphrey was appointed President in his place.

There were changes in the geography of Belfast as well as in the leadership of the Mission, which continued to work with avowed dedication for good and for God amongst its working-class citizens.

By 1960 it had become difficult to define the outer limits of the city.

Continuous building had seen villages such as Dundonald, Finaghy and Glengormley swallowed up into the city boundary. To halt this urban sprawl the Matthews Plan of the early 60's proposed that a Stop Line be drawn with building prohibited outside that line. New housing was to be built in Antrim and Lurgan-Portadown (Craigavon) and city people were to be encouraged to resettle in these areas.

This further migration in population proved a challenge to the organisers of the Belfast City Mission but it was one with which they were well able to cope.

In 1952 a new Hall had been opened on the Shore Road to reach out into the prefabricated bungalows, which had been erected as part of the emergency housing scheme immediately after the War.

Then in the autumn of 1962 the building of a new Hall in Ballysillan on the edge of the new Silverstream housing estate commenced. This Hall was designed to replace the former one in Ligoniel and bring the Gospel message right to the heart of an emergent community. Severe weather during the winter delayed the completion of the project but the new building was eventually dedicated to the work of God in a special service held on Saturday April 6, 1963.

Rev. J. L. Wynne, Minister of Ballysillan Presbyterian Church, gave an appropriate address for a Mission with the aim of reaching out to the people of the district in their home environment. It was based on the words of one of Jesus' final commands to his disciples as recorded in Mark 16:15, 'Go ye into all the world, and preach the gospel to every creature.'

These words were to strike home into the mind of James Davidson who had been transferred in 1952 from Cuba Street on the Newtownards Road to Earl Street, when he was visiting in his second district in the Docks area of the city in the mid-60's.

Different people had told James about Alec Robinson.

"You ought to call and see Alec sometime," they would say. "He lives down near the docks and he is 'a real character'."

James had encountered a few 'real characters' in his time but when he first called with Alec Robinson he was disappointed for he didn't seem to be able to make any headway whatsoever.

"I'm not interested in that kind of thing," was what Alec told him before turning bluntly to walk away.

On telling his friends of the cool reception he had been given by Alec they were a little surprised but thought they knew the answer.

"Did you not ask to see his lion?" they enquired. "He keeps a lion in a cage out the back. Ask to see his lion and see what happens."

A month later James Davidson was back at Alec Robinson's front door. Fearing a further rebuff he began as advised. "They tell me you have a pet lion. Is that right? Is it a big one?" he asked.

Alec's face lit up. The missionary had made a direct hit in his heart.

"It's right, O.K. He's in a cage up the back " Alec responded immediately. "Would you like to see him?"

"I would love to," James said. This was not strictly true for he was not passionately in love with lions, but he recognised the importance of the point of contact.

Alec led the way up though the back yard and out to some rough ground at the rear of the house. On this rough ground there stood what James reckoned to be a rather makeshift looking cage and in that cage there lay a huge lion with a long, tatty mane.

Thankfully it was asleep.

James crept up beside Alec quietly, and stood gazing at the sleeping beast.

He didn't say anything for he was afraid of wakening it up.

All kinds of crazy thoughts rushed through his head. What will happen if that thing gets out of there? he wondered. Then he thought of the verse Rev. Wynne had taken for his text in Ballysillan, and that he had heard used as an exhortation to city missionaries like himself more than once.

'Preach the gospel to *every* creature', it said.

Surely that doesn't stretch to lions, though, he mused, sparing himself an inward chuckle. But I would even have a go at preaching to it if I thought Alec would...

His reverie was broken by Alec stepping forward and banging on the bars of the cage with a paling post. "Come on boy! Wake up, boy!" he began to shout, making as big a racket as possible.

'Boy' as Alec had called him, stirred all of a sudden

He jumped up in the cage and tore at the bars, growling fiercely.

James Davidson prayed silently, "Lord, help me," and stood where he was, trying to appear unconcerned, although the shivers were chasing each other up and down his spine.

"Isn't he powerful?" Alec exclaimed.

"Indeed he is," James felt he had no choice but to agree. It would be a mistake, he reckoned, to disagree with Alec on the subject of lions.

When they had stood for a further few minutes watching the snarling, growling animal pace around its cage as best it could, James thanked Alec for letting him see the lion, but said that he would have to go.

The 'lion-tamer' accompanied the missionary out to the front of the house again and invited him, before he left, to 'call back anytime'.

James was pleased to take Alec at his word and began to call at the house on a regular basis. And now the welcome he received was entirely different to what it had been on his first visit.

"Would you like to read a wee bit to me, and pray before you go, James," Alec began to request. What really pleased James, in addition to being afforded the opportunity to read the scriptures and pray in Alec's home, was the reverence with which this 'character' greeted the reading of the Word of God.

As soon as James opened the Bible Alec slipped the old battered cap off his head and perched it on his knee, and there it stayed until James had said 'Amen' at the close of his prayer. It was then reinstated on Alec's head until the next time.

James persuaded Alec to come around to the Mission Hall one night and many of the locals were surprised to see Alec Robinson in a meeting. Something was going on in Alec's heart, though, that nobody knew about.

A few months after his visit to the Mission Hall Alec became ill and was taken into hospital. James began visiting him and one day he found him unusually bright.

"You look a lot better today, Alec," the missionary began, by way of introduction.

"I feel a lot better, too, James," the patient replied. He placed a wrinkled hand across his heart and went on, "You see a big change has taken place in here."

Alec Robinson had trusted in Christ.

'Preach the gospel to every creature', the Bible said.

James had one scary experience with Alec's lion, and although it would have been pointless preaching to it, the bond of friendship that had been forged with the local 'character' that day, had eventually led to 'a big change having taken place' in his heart.

The time spent visiting Alec Robinson, chatting to him, reading to him and praying with him had all been tremendously and eternally worthwhile.

Every single minute of it.

24

THE GLOOM, THE GLEAM, AND THE GLORY

It is sad when Mission Halls, from which the light of the Gospel had been beamed out into closely-knit local communities for years, are found to be standing right in the middle of the path of that powerful monster, Progress. Yet that is what occurred when the city planners decided to ease the flow of the increasing volume of traffic in and around Belfast by building a road to link the two motorways which had begun to point long fingers of speed out into the countryside. The M1 pierced south into County Down and across through Armagh into Tyrone and the M2 had begun to reach out its grasping tentacles through the northern side of the city towards the fertile fields of County Antrim.

The construction of a 'West Link' to join them both together should be, it was reckoned, of utmost and immediate importance.

The only problem was, however, that this new road was going to cut a swathe through city communities that had been established for years. Hundreds of homes, which had been built in the boom days of the industrial revolution to house the stream of workers flowing in from the country to find jobs in the shipyards and the linen mills, were going to have to be demolished to facilitate this development.

Three Mission Halls would have to go as well.

Earl Street, off York Street, Hutchinson Street, off the Grosvenor Road, and Roden Street off the Donegall Road were all standing directly in the line of the proposed new road, and would have to come down.

Hutchinson Street was first to close. With the scheduled redevelopment planned, and increasing tensions in the district, many people had already moved away from the area and been re-housed in new developments on the fringes of the city. There had been a significant drop in attendances even before the closing service which was held in June 1970. Mr. R. G. Anderson, who had served as missionary in the district for fourteen years was transferred to Derg Street.

By the time the closing service was held in Earl Street in late May 1971 the bulldozers had already moved into the area and what of the houses and tiny shops that had once been the heart of the community life, hadn't been flattened, were already boarded up and scarred by vandalism. The Mission Hall stood, as it had done for years, as a symbol of stability and hope in the middle of a scene of change and desolation. A large number of the people who had lived in the area had been allocated homes in the new housing estates which had been built to replace the prefabricated dwellings which had been so hastily erected after the War. Mr. James Davidson was transferred out from Earl Street to the Shore Road district, where a new Hall was later to be opened in Shore Crescent in 1972.

Four days after the closing service in Earl Street a large crowd packed into the Hall in Roden Street for a similar sort of service. Tributes were paid by many to the valuable contribution the Mission Hall had made to the lives of the people of the district though good times and bad and Miss Mollie Bunting, a lifelong member of the Hall, made a presentation to Mr. Andrew Orr who had been missionary in the district for over eighteen years. Mr. Orr was moved across to the east side of the city to resume his labours for the Lord in Canton Street.

There was not only a shift in population in some of the Belfast districts in the late 60's but also a considerable change in personnel in the City Mission. It seemed that a number of the missionaries all reached retirement age around the same time and younger men were appointed to fill their positions.

Within the space of two years four highly respected men, who between them represented one hundred and fifty eight years service for the Lord in the Mission, retired.

Mr. James Cassidy was the first of them to leave in 1968. He had commenced the work in Kilburn Street and had devoted almost forty years of his life to it, seeing a large number of men, women, boys and girls, led to faith in Christ.

A year later three more senior missionaries retired from active service. Samuel Haslett, who had been appointed in 1926, was nineteen years in Havelock Place, seven in Bellevue Street and sixteen in the Sandy Row district. David Magill was the missionary in Island Street for forty-one years and probably the best-known Christian worker in the Newtownards Road Area. His ready natural wit endeared him to people of all ages and classes in the area. Mr. James Leetch was appointed to Lord Street district in 1933 and over the thirty-six years that followed he maintained a fine and faithful work, seeing many souls won for Christ.

With missionaries retiring, and Halls disappearing, the work of the Belfast City mission didn't grind to a halt, however. The challenge was still there. The non-church going community in the city still needed comfort, companionship and Christ. The answer was to appoint new staff, and build new halls. And that is just what the Mission directors did.

William Cooke was appointed to succeed Mr. Cassidy in Kilburn Street, William Patterson was appointed to succeed Mr. Leetch in Lord Street, and Robert Graham and Ernest Shooter, who had already established his Mission connections by marrying David Magill's daughter, were also appointed as missionaries. These were four younger men with a vision for reaching out to the people of the city with the good news of the Gospel. The work would go on for God, regardless of the changes all around.

In seeking to reach the maximum number of people who had moved out from the city centre to be re-housed, or come in from other areas to work in a number of new factories in the area, the Belfast City Mission established a new Hall in the Rathcoole estate on the north side of the city. Rathcoole was at that time one of the largest estates in the United Kingdom and an ideal centre for reaching a large community for Christ.

This large Hall was opened at a special ceremony on Saturday November 14, 1970. Every seat in the spacious building was occupied that day, as the Hall was dedicated to the service of God in Rathcoole. The Hall was declared open by Miss May Morgan and Rev. John Girvan gave an appropriate address on the text 'The glory of the Lord filled the house'. 2 Chron.7:2.

When the new missionary in the district, Robert Graham, had been introduced he spoke of the anticipated problems and pleasures of the task ahead, concluding his remarks with what amounted to a personal prayer. "I feel that the Mission has a great work to do for God in Rathcoole," he said. "May God give to us the strength and wisdom needed that we may see His Kingdom extended in this rapidly developing district."

That prayer for strength, wisdom and the blessing of God in the work was answered for within two years the Mission Hall in Rathcoole had begun to make a significant impact in the area. It was open every night of the week with a full programme of meetings and activities designed to reach the residents of the huge estate with the news of God's redeeming grace.

The Sunday School had over two hundred pupils who were taught by twenty-five teachers every Sabbath afternoon. The formation of a Boy's Brigade Company opened up a new avenue for evangelism with more than seventy boys between the ages of eight and seventeen attending every week. At a B.B. camp in Scotland in the summer of 1972 a number of these lads committed their lives to Christ.

A Girl's group met every Monday evening and special meetings were arranged to cater particularly for men, women and senior citizens.

A worthwhile witness for God had been established to work in conjunction with other evangelical church groups in Rathcoole.

Back in the older Halls the work continued as before with new missionaries setting about their work with a will.

William Cooke had become a well-known visitor around the large Kilburn Street district when he received a telephone call one

September evening. His wife and he were preparing to retire for the night when the phone rang just after eleven o'clock. The caller, who identified himself as having come to the Mission Hall a number of times, sounded quite upset. His father was in hospital.

"Mr. Cooke," came the request, "My father is critically ill in the City Hospital and it is doubtful if he will make it through the night. Is there any chance that you could go and have a talk with him?"

Billy Cooke didn't need a second invitation to go and visit someone and tell them about the Saviour, whoever, or wherever, they were.

"Don't worry," he assured the concerned son. "I'll be there soon."

What he didn't know, however, was that his car would refuse to start when he went out to it. No matter how hard he tried he couldn't get a single kick from the engine. The thing just wasn't going to go. That was it.

The missionary had given his word, and so he set off into the night, walking to the Belfast City Hospital at least two miles away.

It was all worth it though, for in the silent watches of the night he led that dying man to faith in Christ. Billy Cooke walked it all the way home again happy in the knowledge that the man he had spoken to was ready to meet God, with his soul saved and his sins forgiven.

The man did survive the night, but a few days later he passed into the presence of the Lord whom he had just come to know, and his family became more regular in their attendance in Kilburn Street.

1971 saw the retirement of two men who had spent many years in the service of the mission. The first of these was Rev. David Porter who had held the office of Honorary Secretary for fourteen years. Rev. John Girvan, the former city missionary who had been so highly respected in the Donegall Road district, and who had left in order to train for the Presbyterian ministry, was appointed to the position in his place.

The other man was John Cunningham, who had commenced his work with the Mission in the Sandy Row district in May 1915. After five years there he was transferred to Canton Street in east Belfast where he served the Lord and the community for fifty-one years.

At a presentation evening in the Canton Street Hall on Friday May 21, 1971, many tributes were paid to the work of John

Cunningham and his enduring legacy for God and the Gospel in the area.

In reply to all the kind compliments Mr. Cunningham reflected on his fifty-six years with the Belfast City Mission in a talk, which he called, 'The Gloom, The Gleam and The Glory.'

The ageing missionary began by telling of how, when he had commenced his service for the Lord in Sandy Row, it had been against the backdrop of a World War, political unrest, and a devastating flu epidemic.

He went on to relate how the gleam began to pierce the gloom in Canton Street, when he had conducted a Gospel mission in 1921 and God graciously manifested His power in salvation, with many deciding for Christ.

During the days of unemployment and depression in the 30's he had been involved in helping administer the Lord Mayor's Relief Fund, thus helping the gleam to penetrate a further period of gloom.

The glory to which he referred was the joy of seeing lives transformed through faith in Christ, and new Christians going on to live and witness for God in the district.

He recounted the story of a man who in his early day had no time for either the missionary or the Gospel message. When his family had disowned him and evicted him from the house because of a life of continual drunkenness and abuse, however, John Cunningham had found him lying drunk and injured on the pavement one night. The missionary arranged for the outcast to be taken to hospital and treated, and began to visit him.

As he continued to demonstrate practical Christian love and share the glad news of salvation and pardon through trusting Jesus, with one who had once been so antagonistic, John had noticed a certain mellowing in his attitude. In less than a year this man had found Christ as Saviour and immediately began to tell others of the peace and rest he had found in life at last.

That was the kind of glory that delighted John Cunningham's heart. It was the glory of the Lord, gleaming out through the gloom in the world around, from the life of a believer.

Over the cup of tea that followed that evening, the big crowd, many of whom had known John Cunningham from childhood days in the Sunday School, shared with the retiring missionary and his wife, and with each other, some of the other incidents they remembered. These were events that the modest missionary hadn't mentioned in his Gloom, Gleam and Glory review.

There was the Canton Street Mixed Choir and the lantern slideshows they often staged at other Halls across the city. The choir sang and then John Cunningham showed his lantern slides illustrating a well-known story. 'Uncle Tom's Cabin' was a great favourite. These meetings were usually packed with the congregations reckoning that they had given good value for money. The sixpence admission fee included supper!

Some recalled the death of Malcolm Murray, a local drunkard. When this man, who had virtually lived on the streets around the district, passed away, news spread around that since he had no relatives to look after his affairs he was to be buried in a pauper's grave.

"That will not happen," John Cunningham told someone, and he arranged his funeral, buying a coffin and procuring a plot in a graveyard. That act of kindness in the community did much to bring people into the Hall in Canton Street.

Others remembered the dark, hungry days of the thirties, when food parcels would appear, mysteriously and anonymously, at homes where money was in extremely short supply and regular, wholesome meals were considered a luxury. The only clue that anyone could connect with the origin of these parcels was that John Cunningham had called at the house the day before.

Even after his retirement John Cunningham continued to be involved in social work in the district and in 1978 he was award the M.B.E. for having helped organise the meals-on-wheels scheme in his east Belfast district for more than twenty years.

Population redistribution in the city was to result in the closure of another Mission Hall, that in McClure Street, off the Ormeau Road, in 1974. At the closing service in September of that year, Mr. William Lynas, who, although he had earlier retired, was invited to return and recollect something of his forty years service in the Hall.

He, too, was able to tell of the work in difficult days, of the Lord Mayor's relief Fund and the collections of clothes made by the congregation of Fitzroy Presbyterian Church. These clothes were much appreciated by the needy families whom he had contacted.

On a lighter note there were many knowing nods of the head amongst some of the men present when William Lynas recalled the holidays he arranged for the boys of the McClure Street district in Keenan's barn off the Main Street in Ballywalter, Co Down.

One of the most rewarding aspects of the work in Mc Clure Street, as he looked back, was the fact that eight young men who had come to faith, and had received their early experience in public speaking in the Hall, had gone on to train for the ministry of the Church. Two of these men were at that time serving in America, two others were in Scotland and the remaining two in the province. There was an even more thrilling personal ingredient to this encouraging reminiscence as well. The two ministering in churches in Northern Ireland were his own sons, Victor and Cowper!

As John Cunningham had said, his work for God had allowed him to witness gleams of glory perforating days and years of gloom.

Yet a gloom, in the form of the stalking spectre of death and destruction had descended upon the province in the early 70's.

Could the light of the glory of God punch any holes in IT?

25

BULLETS, BOMBS AND BARRICADES

In the early years of the 1970's many parts of Belfast became caught up in the throes of bitter civil and paramilitary strife. Loyalist and republican gunmen and bombers confronted each other and, or, the British Army and, or, the Royal Ulster Constabulary, both of whom had been assigned the task of restoring that elusive quality, 'law and order'.

Days and nights of rioting and high tension followed one another for weeks, particularly, but not exclusively, in the north and west of the city. Bullets flew, bombs exploded, barricades were erected, and people on each and every side were killed or injured.

Caught up in the middle of all this were the majority of the ordinary, decent, hard-working men and women of the city who wanted nothing more than to be left in peace to live in peace.

When the trouble was at its worst, the missionaries, Halls and workers of the Belfast City Mission became involved with assisting these people in whatever way they could. They had no option.

For years the message that God cared deeply for everybody, and because God cared the Mission cared, had been taught and demonstrated on the streets and in the Halls. The little Halls that had stood so silently, so unobtrusively, in side streets, were soon to be used as havens of refuge. It was not uncommon for the Mayo Street minibus to be loaded up with as much of the contents of a house as it could hold in the middle of the night, rescuing a terrified family from an embattled street in a strife-torn neighbourhood. This furniture would then be stored in the Mission Hall until a new home could be found for the family.

Mayo Street Hall was sited in a strategic position, close to the Peace Line between the Falls and Shankill Roads, and the missionary there, Colin McFarland, occasionally found himself caught up in the situation. He had come to the area to tell the people about the love of God, but when those people were in fear for their lives, he often had to intervene on their behalf.

One night in August 1971, Colin and a man who he had led to the Lord about a year before in the Hall, were called upon to act as intermediaries in what looked like developing into a very ugly confrontation.

Loyalists from the Shankill Road were objecting to republicans from the Falls driving across Ainsworth Avenue to cause trouble in their neighbourhoods. The Ulster Defence Association had come out on to Ainsworth Avenue in large numbers and had issued what seemed to amount to an ultimatum to the officer commanding the Army. Reduced to simple terms it meant, 'If you don't do something about this we will, and you won't stop us.'

A number of the local people asked the city missionary and the man from the Hall who knew some of the local men involved, to attempt to talk to both the U.D.A. and the Army, to see if they could help broker a deal to avoid bloodshed. After a certain amount of flitting to and fro they arranged for the Army commander and leading representatives of the U.D.A. to meet in the Christian's house in Mayo Street, just down from the Hall.

It was tense.

Colin knew that the Bible said, 'Blessed are the peacemakers: for they shall be called the children of God.' That was all very well to say, but he was also acutely aware that feelings were running very high in the street outside. If an agreement wasn't reached there could be a serious loss of life.

When the two sides had been brought together in the home, Colin and his friend slipped surreptitiously into the shadows to allow them to talk. They had done all they could do on the ground. All that remained for them to do now was pray.

It worked. Eventually.

The prayers, not only of the missionary and the household host of the high-powered negotiations, but also of all the Christians who knew that they were taking place, were answered.

A measure of peace was restored, for a short time at least.

Breathing space had been bought.

The profile of the Mission in the district had been greatly enhanced, also, and the missionary had been afforded opportunities to speak to men who wouldn't normally have had any time for God or spiritual concerns.

Just a month later, on the evening of September 13, 1971, across in Hillview Street Mission Hall in the Crumlin Road area of the city, Dennis Bannerman, a new young missionary, was introduced as an assistant to Mr. John Luke, who had served in the district for more than twenty years.

Mr. David Hamilton, General Secretary of the Mission, had taken part in the meeting, and as he lived in the vicinity declined all offers of 'a lift home' when the service was over, preferring to walk.

He had just left and Dennis was chatting to John Luke and a few other friends who had remained behind to help clear up in the Hall when a mighty explosion rocked the building.

A bomb had exploded at the top of Buller Street, not far away.

Everybody's thoughts turned instantly to David.

"That's the way he would go, up Buller Street," a man who knew the locality well said, in a spontaneous expression of concern.

The Hall was immediately locked up and John and Dennis hurried off in the direction of the blast. It was natural in such situations to expect the worst but the two missionaries were pleased, on arriving at the scene of the explosion, to discover that David was alive and well.

God had given His angels charge over him.

He had been just a few hundred yards from the bomb when it went off, but although covered in dust and grime he had come through it relatively unscathed. The blast, however, had caused extensive structural damage to a grocery store and the bakery next door.

When the two panting missionaries came upon their General Secretary he was doing his duty as a good Christian citizen. David Hamilton had armed himself with a sturdy plank of wood from the shattered buildings and he was preventing a group of local youngsters from looting the grocer's shop until the police and Army took control!

Hundreds of homes in Hillview Street, Buller Street, and other streets in the vicinity of the bomb had suffered shattered windows and minor structural damage in the blast. John Luke and Dennis Bannerman kept their Testaments and tracts in their pockets and equipped themselves with hammers and hardboard as they helped the local residents to effect temporary repairs. This allowed them to spend times in homes, and speak to appreciative people, for as long as it took them to carry out the work.

The Mission Hall in Hillview Street doubled as a hardboard store and distribution centre for the emergency repair teams from the Housing Trust. The spirit of the people in the district was indomitable, and the companionship created out of crisis in those days helped the missionaries to make and maintain vital contact with them.

In early March 1972,Dennis Bannerman moved to become the missionary in charge of the Hall in Jersey Street in the Shankill Road area. His experience in Hillview Street proved invaluable in his new district. For it was just more of the same.

He had only been leading the mission there for about six weeks when the Hall became surrounded by gunmen firing at each other on the night of the mid-week meeting. It would be dangerous for anyone to go out on the streets so those present remained in the Hall until the shooting subsided. Then, when they considered it safe, Dennis and a number of the senior workers escorted groups of those who had been present, home. They left at intervals by the back door and walked by side streets and circuitous routes to their different destinations.

In the summer of that year Dennis received a distress call from a family who attended the Hall. The two sisters lived with their elderly father in a lovely flat in the Springmartin estate on the outskirts of the city.

On the night when they called the gunfire around them had become so frightening that they were afraid for their lives.

"Please Dennis, can you do something for us?" was their plea. "Can you get us out of here? We are going to be killed, or at least driven out of our flat onto the street if we stay."

Dennis reacted immediately. He borrowed a van from someone he knew and solicited the help of John Parkes, one of the senior workers in Jersey Street. The two men then set off, under cover of darkness, and with gunfire still cracking in the air around them.

Working feverishly, they loaded as much of the family's furniture as they could possibly cram into the van, taking care to leave space for five people on the exit run. It was with tears in their eyes when they thought of the past, and fear in their hearts as they contemplated an uncertain future, that those two ladies and their father left the home in which they had spent much of their lives.

The missionary drove down to Jersey Street Hall and there they unloaded the family furniture for safe keeping until a new home could be found for them in a safer area. John Parkes took the man and his daughters to his home for the remainder of that night, and then arranged accommodation for them with others from the Hall in the days that followed.

The story didn't end there, though. The family needed a new home.

Dennis contacted the local M.P. Mr. John McQuade and they joined forces in striving to find somewhere for the three to live. When the two men heard of a house that had become vacant in a more suitable area of the city, John McQuade went down to the Housing Trust office and said that he was sitting there until he was given the rent book for it.

He got it too!

Another district that was right at the heart of the strife in the city was that around the Hall in Ardglen where Mr. Tom Forbes had worked for God, with the local population for over thirty years.

In his area Tom Forbes heard of a woman who had suffered a horrible injury.

When she heard that there were children throwing stones at the security forces this concerned mother went out to bring in her two younger children, a boy of nine and a girl of six. Just as she retuned to her own home a canister of C.S. gas exploded at her feet, leaving her severely burned.

On hearing this story from one of her neighbours Tom Forbes began to visit her in hospital, thus establishing contact with the family. When the lady was discharged from hospital he began to visit in the home and soon the family began to attend the services in the Mission Hall.

At Christmas Tom was touched. He called round at the home one day with a toy for each of the children and a box of groceries for their parents, and on his way out the husband and father spoke to him in the hall of the little kitchen house.

"I want to thank you for all you have done for us, Mr. Forbes," he said. "We used to think, with all this bitterness and hate around us, that all the love had gone out of the world, but you have shown us that it hasn't. Thank God for all the kind men and women in the Mission who actually care for people like us."

The Ardglen Hall didn't survive the seventies. It was severely damaged by a bomb at a nearby shop in February 1973 and in 1976 it was completely destroyed by fire.

The Troubles disrupted life in a number of areas of the city for a vast number of people, and yet they also gave the missionaries an opportunity to visit both families and individuals, showing them the love of Christ in a very practical way. Many were led to faith in Christ through their caring ministry.

Some of the missionaries risked their own lives in those days, for the sake of the Christian Gospel, yet they didn't look upon their actions as anything special, or different, or heroic. They had been called of God to serve Him in a situation, and this is what they saw themselves doing, no matter what the circumstances.

The real heroes of those tough times were the ordinary people, the men, women and children who carried on with life as normal, surmounting endless obstacles with never a murmur.

This steely spark was demonstrated one evening when Dennis Bannerman welcomed a little old lady who had walked to the mid-week meeting in Jersey Street Mission Hall, despite serious rioting in the streets all around.

"Great to see you Mrs. Aitch," the missionary greeted her," but did you not think of staying at home with all this going on?"

"Son," came the old lady's reply, as she looked Dennis straight in the eye, "nothing will stop me coming to worship the Lord! Hitler couldn't do it with his bombs in the blitz, and nobody, or nothing, is going to do it now!"

26

JOSS

Every year was significant in the history of the Belfast City Mission for in every year since it was established its missionaries, workers, Sunday School teachers and leaders of youth organisations have seen many people of all ages commit their lives to Christ. That has always been the ultimate goal of the Mission and hence it must ever be its most telling statistic.

However, 1977 was notable in its own particular way for that was when the Belfast City Mission celebrated it 150th anniversary. In the annual report for the year the secretary summed up a brief historical outline he had given of the work of the Mission over a century and a half with the words,

> 'Only eternity will reveal the true results of a ministry that has been shared by a multitude of dedicated workers throughout the years, men of God who, like those who inaugurated the work, had a passion for the souls of people and an earnest desire to win them for their Saviour. Such a spirit of compassion and love for the lost constrains us still. This report makes it evident that there is still sufficient need to justify the continuance of the work and resulting blessing assures

us that God still has a purpose and plan for it in the
needy places in the city.'

The 'spirit of compassion and love for the lost' which was
displayed by the missionaries in their visits from street to street and
those who organised and led the meetings in the Halls, was often
very much appreciated by the community amongst whom they
worked. They demonstrated this, too, when the occasion arose.

1977 was remembered not only because of the 150th anniversary,
but also because that was the year in which the Hall in Jersey Street
was completely destroyed by fire. A street bonfire nearby blazed out
of control setting the Hall alight and burning it to the ground.

This tragedy provoked widespread sympathy for the missionary
and those who assisted him, from the local residents, and many
voluntary collections were made in the area to help restore the Hall.
In the course of six months almost five thousand pounds in donations
from these spontaneous collecting agencies, and personal gifts, had
been received in the Mission office. Alternative accommodation was
also made available in the district so that the work of the Mission
could carry on until the original building had been restored.

This renovation and restoration work took almost a year to
complete and the new Hall was opened in April 1978.

Although the missionaries are responsible for the overall
organisation of the outreach in their individual districts much of the
groundwork in their Halls is carried out by ordinary, often unsung,
men and women 'with a passion for the souls of people'. Their work,
too, is often very much appreciated, but sadly often not until they
are not there to do it any longer.

Lily Boal was a lady like that.

When she returned from serving the Lord as a missionary with
W.E.C. in the late 70's, Lily was asked to start a ladies' prayer meeting
in Mountcollyer Mission Hall. She did this willingly, and a few years
later she began an outreach meeting for the women of the district.

This godly lady, with her gentle caring nature was greatly loved
by the women who came to the meeting, and Lily had the thrill of
personally leading many of them to Christ. She also became a trusted
confidante to many and when some of the ladies had a problem about
anything they always seemed happy to ask Lily for advice.

Having spearheaded this simple meeting for almost ten years she was forced to retire because of failing health, and in less than six months she had passed into the presence of the Master she had served so faithfully.

A huge crowd braved a very wet day to attend her funeral in Mountcollyer Mission Hall, and amongst the crowd there were women who said softly, "Lily Boal showed me what true Christian love was like." Others testified quite simply, "It was Lily who led me to the Lord."

With the ongoing emphasis on building new houses on the outskirts of the city, many people who had lived for half a lifetime in the streets of east Belfast moved out to occupy new homes in the large estate under construction at Ballybeen. As with Rathcoole on the city's north side, so also with this mushrooming community of almost ten thousand residents on its eastern boundary.

The men of vision in the Belfast City Mission realised that it would be an ideal location in which to site a Mission Hall. It represented a tremendous opportunity to reach thousands of people with the truth of the Gospel.

After a period of planning and building a new Hall was opened on the estate in March 1976. Mr. Ernest Shooter, who had spent his first eight years with the Mission in East Bread Street, was moved four or five miles out the Newtownards Road to lead this venture of faith and evangelism in Ballybeen.

Initial systematic visitation across the estate brought promising results. People, some of whom had no church connections whatsoever, began to come occasionally to the services. Right from the Hall opened, though, one of the singularly most encouraging facets of the work in Ballybeen was the number of children and young people attending the Sunday School.

This interest amongst the young led Ernie Shooter to have an increasing burden for the number of teenagers in the estate who complained of having nothing to do, or nowhere to go, in the evenings. Wouldn't it be wonderful, he reasoned, if we could see these young people attracted to the Hall, and more importantly, won for Christ?

He could read the mindset of many of them. They were a band of teenagers who considered themselves too old for Sunday School and yet too young and 'with-it' to sit in Sunday evening services with rows of middle-aged Christian 'squares'.

Appealing youth organisations, based in a specially designed youth hall or centre, and led by committed Christian men and women, were what was needed. When he had identified this particular need Ernie Shooter didn't sit about on his hands. He took steps to put his vision into practice.

Many from the Hall and district, who shared his concern for the youth of the estate, helped where they could in the construction of a specifically equipped Youth Hall, which was opened in 1979.

The Boys Brigade and Girls Brigade Companies, which had already been formed in the Mission Hall, moved into this purpose built facility, and blossomed. It seemed to be just what not only many of the young people, but also the parents, of the district had been wanting.

A team of dedicated leaders helped the missionary to set up well-drilled, well-organised Boys and Girls Brigade Companies and these were soon to prove spiritually profitable in a couple of ways.

In the first instance they afforded an opportunity for the presentation of the Gospel message to the young people and many of them gave their lives to the Lord, especially in the summer camps. Secondly, it allowed the leaders of the organisations to contact a large number of parents, many of whom would never enter a place of worship. In one particular G.B. enrolment service in the early 80's, six mothers sat along in a row at the front and every single one of their husbands, or 'partners', was in prison, convicted of offences relating to paramilitary activity.

Although the work amongst the young in Ballybeen continued to reap rich spiritual returns, it was only one aspect of an extensive outreach to a big estate. The missionary to the district carried on a methodical programme of visitation on a day-to-day basis and it was through responding to a request for a visit to an ill man that he saw an interesting character brought to Christ.

It was late on a Tuesday evening when Ernie Shooter had a phone call from a lady who was obviously worried. When she gave her name the missionary recognised her. She had been along at the Hall once or twice on special occasions.

"My husband would like to see you, Mr. Shooter, some day. He is very ill and he says he would like to talk to you," she said.

"Don't worry, I will be round tomorrow morning," the missionary promised, sensing that the lady was extremely concerned.

Having noted the address, Ernie Shooter called at the house the following morning to be greeted by Joss, a man who was not renowned for his sympathy for anything remotely religious, and a leading 'pigeon man'. Joss bred and raced prize-winning homing pigeons and for years all the activity of his entire leisure time had been centred around his 'loft'.

Joss hadn't sent for Ernie to talk about pigeons, though. He had weightier matters on his mind.

"What's the trouble, Joss? How can I help you?" the missionary enquired after the initial introductions had been dispensed with.

"My problem is that I have got cancer, Mr. Shooter. I have been told that there is little hope for me," Joss blurted out, all in a torrent. "And the truth of the matter is, I am not ready to meet God."

It was the fearful, frank confession of a man staring the prospect of entering eternity, and of meeting God, fair in the face.

Ernie Shooter understood the fear of a death without hope, but he had the solution to the situation. He slipped his little New Testament from his pocket, and read a few verses that illustrated the truth of the Gospel, how that Christ, by His death on Calvary had made provision for men like Joss. As the critically ill man listened attentively, the missionary then went on to explain the way of salvation to him.

When he had finished Joss was amazed at the simplicity of it all. "You mean if I ask Jesus to forgive my sins and come into my heart and be my Saviour He will do it? Is it as easy as that?" he asked, a trifle puzzled.

"Yes, that's what I mean," Ernie went on to assure him. "Salvation comes free to all those who call upon the Lord. But remember it was bought at a terrible price. It cost Jesus His life to atone for us."

Joss was moved by the love of God for Him and said simply, "I'm going to trust Him now."

And bowing his head, he did.

The news that Joss had turned 'good-livin'' rocked the pigeon fraternity, but the rumour that he was putting his entire stock of award-winning pigeons, and his loft, up for sale caused an even bigger stir.

Men flocked to his home from all parts of Belfast, anxious to buy one or two good breeding pairs. Before they were sold anything, however, they had to sit and listen to Joss telling them why they were being allowed to buy them. He was going to die, but he wasn't afraid to die, for he had made his peace with God. He was a Christian now.

When it came to the disposal of the final item to go, the pigeon shed in which Joss had idled away so many of the hours of his life, the seller had one specific condition of sale.

"The man who buys it must promise me that he won't take it down on a Sunday!" was his single stipulation. "You see I am a Christian now, and if I'm well enough at all I will be out at Church!"

Ernie Shooter made it part of his policy to visit Joss on a regular basis and one day he found that the new convert had a special request to make.

"Mr. Shooter, I have wasted so much of my life, but now I am happy in Christ. I would love to do something for God if I could," he began, and then hesitated with the sort of long pause that signifies a response of some sort is expected.

"And what had you in mind, Joss," Ernie wanted to know.

"I was wondering if I could stand at the door of the Hall and give out the hymn-books for a week or two?" Joss replied softly, rather embarrassed. "When I come to think about it, there really isn't much else that I could do."

When Ernie told the others back at the Hall of that simple request the men who normally stood at the door to welcome the incoming congregation on a Sunday evening were delighted to be able to allow Joss his wish.

All who came were touched by the warmth of the welcome he gave them, but Joss was only able to do that job for four Sundays. It was then that the disease took control of his body, leaving him so weak that he was unable to leave his home, or his bed.

In eleven weeks from the Wednesday morning when Ernie Shooter had led him to the Lord, Joss died without fear. He was ready to meet God, and the testimony he left behind amongst the pigeon-men of the city, and the residents of Ballybeen, was talked about for months.

Stories like this, of the power of God to transform a life, could be told, albeit with a change of characters and circumstances, but with the same glorious end result, from each of the Mission districts down the years.

The responsibility for the smooth running of such a spiritually productive organisation needed to be in a sensible, capable man. In David Hamilton, who had been General Secretary for twenty-three years before retiring in 1983, the Mission had been privileged to have someone who proved himself able for the task. He was a man skilled in dealing both with personnel and finance, with missionaries and with money.

Paying tribute to him on his retirement, Rev. Dr. John Girvan, Honorary Secretary of the Mission said,

> 'After twenty-three years in the position of General Secretary, the latter half of which covered the period of economic depression and increasing unemployment, not to mention the continuing disorder in the city, causing deep distress and unhappiness, it has been abundantly proved that Mr. Hamilton's appointment was inspired by God Himself. In his supervision and oversight of the Staff he exercised the utmost consideration, thereby winning the confidence and esteem of every missionary...'

The fact that the annual income to the Mission increased more than sevenfold in his twenty-three years in office demonstrates something of his skill in making known the increasing financial considerations of the organisation with so many new Halls being built, and in overseeing the income and expenditure accounts with a keen business eye.

Mr. Hamilton was succeeded as General Secretary by Mr. William Cooke who had been his Assistant for nine years. He too was a man who knew what it was like to serve God as a missionary on the streets of the city and he was possessed by an overriding desire to see men and women won for Christ.

And that was what mattered most.

27

TO GIVE LIGHT TO THEM THAT SIT IN DARKNESS

For many of the thousands of residents of the scores of small streets that radiate off the main roads leading out of the city, the Belfast City Mission Hall was a landmark, an institution.

This came to light very forcibly when the Housing Executive made public its intention to apply for a vesting order to have the Island Street Hall, with a number of the outdated dwellings around it, demolished, in order to make way for a more modern housing development.

Those who had attended the Hall, many of them from childhood, were upset.

'We want to keep God in our street,' one protestor told a local newspaper. 'There has been a Mission Hall in this district for more than a hundred years and we want it to stay.'

In order to prove the sentimental and spiritual significance of the building, a group of worried residents invited a photographer from the paper to take a picture of a plaque on the wall, which stated,

In memory of SAMUEL ALEXANDER BILL, M.B.E.
Founder of the QUA IBOE MISSION

His work for his Master began in this Hall, which his
father built.
He sailed for Africa in 1887 and died there in the service
of the Qua Iboe Mission 24 th January 1942.
'To give light to them that sit in darkness.'

The concern of the locals was shared by the Board of the Mission
and they negotiated with the Housing Executive for the purchase of
a nearby site. This agreement satisfied the people from the area
who had been so perturbed. Then, when a new building was erected
with space allocated on one of its walls for the memorial plaque to
be displayed, they were happy again. After all they now had a modern,
purpose built Hall in which to praise the Lord, and from which to
reach out to the surrounding community. Mr. Samuel Morrow was
the missionary appointed to lead the work in the new Island Street
Hall, following the retirement of Mr. Robert Jess.

The building was declared open on Saturday October 29, 1988,
by Mrs. Montgomery, wife of the president, Dr. D.A.D. Montgomery
who acted as chairman for the proceedings.

The work of the Lord in the Mission continued to progress across
the city in the late 1980's and into the 90's with regular door to door
visitation taking place and occasional evangelical campaigns being
conducted in various districts. In 1988 the members of the Bilston
Road Hall in Ballysillan celebrated the 25th anniversary of the
opening of their Hall with a two-week Gospel campaign in April.
The evangelist was Mr. Philip Campbell and over the period a number
of people committed their lives to the Lord.

One man, for whom the Christians had been praying very
earnestly, arrived round at the home of Mr. Arthur McClelland, who
was missionary in the district at the time, about an hour after the
final meeting of the mission.

"Mr. McClelland," he began, in a state of obvious anxiety. " I
feel I can't go to bed tonight without settling this matter of my soul's
salvation."

The missionary invited him in, and had the joy, in a short space
of time, of leading him to Christ. The seeking soul had found the

Saviour.

On the other side of the city, in Canton Street, a very fruitful mission was held in 1994. Before the campaign began, the Christians from the Hall gathered regularly to pray for God's blessing in salvation. In early morning prayer meetings on a Saturday they poured out their hearts to the Lord for a powerful 'movement of the Holy Spirit' in the district. They then undertook to visit every home in the area, personally inviting people to come along.

When the opening night arrived, Bobi Brown the missionary, and those who had helped him organise the mission were not disappointed, either in the numbers attending or with the simple and straightforward way in which Rev. Stephen Dickinson presented the Gospel.

Over the two weeks of the meetings many people, including quite a number of who had never been in the Hall before, came, and by the end of the fortnight six people had come to Christ.

God had heard the prayers of his people, and had responded in a mighty manner. For such answers those people were the first to return Him the praise.

In the early 90's a difficult decision had to be made in relation to the old wooden hall which had served as a base for the activities of the Belfast City Mission in Great Northern Street since 1934. It was beyond repair and would have to be demolished.

Mr Robert Anderson had served the Lord faithfully as missionary to the district in that building for fifty-two years. In his more than half a century of dedicated ministry he had helped needy people through all kinds of hardship, and had seen many people, both young and old, converted. In all his work Mr. Anderson had enjoyed the active support of his wife and family to such an extent that the Hall in Great Northern Street in south Belfast was affectionately known to some simply as 'Andersons.'

Mr. Ian Harbinson was appointed as Mr. Anderson's successor when the senior missionary retired in 1986, and when Ian left to study for the Presbyterian ministry in 1993, Mr. Ronnie Mc Cullough took his place.

The new missionary began his work in the district using the Ulsterville Presbyterian Church Hall in Lorne Street as his operational base. Although he was without a specific building in which to work, Ronnie was never short of work to do. There were so many people to visit, both around the doors in the district and in the two large Hospitals nearby.

One of the first people Ronnie had the privilege of pointing to the Saviour in his new district was a man who was critically ill in the City Hospital.

Sammy had once run a small business in Belfast, but one day he was tied up and robbed in his shop. This had a detrimental effect on his health and some years later he suffered a severe stroke.

His physical condition continued to deteriorate and his sister, who attended the Mission Hall fellowship and was concerned about her brother's spiritual condition asked Ronnie to go and visit him.

It was a Monday morning when the missionary first called to see Sammy but found him unable to communicate owing to his condition. Ronnie introduced himself to Sammy and the anxious family at the bedside, then prayed and left.

On Wednesday he returned, and finding Sammy alone, with the screens around his bed, he spoke to him simply and briefly about the need to trust the Saviour. He then prayed again, and left.

At the Thursday evening service Sammy's sister told Ronnie that her brother had passed away, but before he died he had told her, as best he could, that he was trusting in Jesus.

What an encouragement to a Christian sister in a time of sorrow, and to a City missionary in a time of apparently endless, fruitless routine work.

Ronnie was soon to have a new centre from which to serve the Lord, too, for in May 1995 a building in the area, close to where the old Hall had been, was bought. With the willing help of a number of volunteers from the area the building was then converted, ready to live a new life as an outpost of the Belfast City Mission.

All this valuable work had been going on in the Halls and under the auspices of the Mission, against a continuing backdrop of armed confrontation both in the city and the provincial towns of Northern Ireland. Civilians, members of the Army and the police force, and paramilitary activists on both sides had all lost their lives or sustained horrific injuries in the ongoing conflict.

When everyone thought that 'things couldn't get any worse', they invariably did. One act of carnage seemed to follow another with sickening regularity.

One incident which brought home to the people of Belfast the utter futility of it all was the no-warning bomb in Frizell's fish shop on the Shankill Road on October 23, 1993. Ten people, nine innocent Saturday afternoon shoppers and one of the bombers were killed that day, and fifty-eight others were injured.

The missionaries of the Belfast City Mission in a number of the Halls around the Shankill became immediately involved in the aftermath of that bomb, doing what they could to comfort grieving relatives, and visiting many of those who had been injured, both in hospital and in their homes.

Three of those who died were from the same family. They were a father, mother and their little daughter who had attended the Sunday School in the Glencairn Mission Hall. On the day of the massive funeral the missionary and workers from the Hall provided a tea for all the grieving relatives and their friends and the Hall was packed as more than one hundred grateful people responded to their invitation.

The visits of the missionaries in the area, and the many tender acts of kindness and care that were demonstrated at that time, helped show the Mission as a group which cared deeply for the people of the district in all the situations of life. It showed that they served a Master who was always touched by compassion for unhappy, hungry multitudes, and who, when His friend died, took the time to stand outside his grave and weep with his sisters before raising him from the dead.

It was in 1988 that the City Mission took to the country again. Since it was forty years since David Hamilton's memorable mission in Carnalbanagh, the local Presbyterian Church invited them to send a team to mark the anniversary by conducting an intensive evangelistic outreach in the area. Four missionaries, Bobbi Brown, Robin Fairbairn, Johnston Lambe and Errol McCrory, four of the younger missionaries, were asked to leave their Halls in the charge of others for two weeks and spend two weeks in the country. They worked hard at it, visiting every house in the village and all the scattered farms for miles around, sharing the Gospel with those who would listen, and inviting people along to the evening services in the Presbyterian Church.

These meetings did not have the same impact on the countryside as the previous mission forty years before. Some souls were won for the Lord and this was a blessing and an answer to prayer, but that campaign in Carnalbanagh had an indirect, but appreciable, effect on the further operation of the outreach of the Mission.

It appeared to act as a catalyst to kick-start other missions amongst rural congregations. Seemingly it had renewed a recognition, amongst the Presbyterian Church across the province, of the Belfast City Mission and its dedicated missionaries, as a powerful agency for evangelism.

A renewed emphasis on outreach evangelism was just one of a number of changes that the leadership of the Mission felt it necessary to make as they approached the end of the twentieth century.

Times were changing.

Sunday School numbers were dropping as a general rule, and with all the comforts and conveniences of modern living the missionaries were finding it increasingly difficult to attract unsaved people to the meetings in the little hall up the street, or round the corner.

Some prayerful consideration would have to be given to such matters.

And some hard, practical thinking would have to be done.

How best could the City Mission achieve its aim of reaching out to people in Belfast in an age that seemed to bring out some new electronic gadget for their pleasure every six months or so, and yet an age in which every technological step forward seemed to be off-set by two moral steps back?

Although everything seemed to be in a state of rapid flux, one factor remained as an eternal constant.

God hadn't changed. He was, is, and ever will be the same.

And He would show the way

28

I'LL MAYBE COME ON SUNDAY

The challenges of the turn of the century were to be undertaken by a new management team at the Mission. These men would be responsible for all the spiritual and practical implications of the day-to-day running of its increasing variety of outreach operations.

Mr. William Cooke, who had been General Secretary through seven troubled years in the history of Belfast, was forced to retire owing to ill health in 1990.

Mr. Johnston Lambe, who had served as Mr. Cooke's assistant for six years was appointed to the position in his place, with Mr. Robin Fairbairn as his assistant.

Like all the previous secretaries before him, Johnston came to the job with years of experience of Mission work behind him. He had committed his life to the Lord in Rathcoole Hall under the ministry of Mr. Roy Graham. Johnston then progressed to helping with all the various aspects of evangelism in Rathcoole before joining the Mission as a full-time worker and assistant to the senior missionary in his home district in 1978. A year later he was transferred to take charge of the work in Shore Crescent.

During his six-year period there he saw a number come to faith in Christ and he also learnt much about the practical nature of the

Christian ministry. He counted it a privilege to serve God in the company of mature believers like David and Betty Currie, who, with others, acted as spiritual mentors to the young, enthusiastic missionary.

When he had served three years as General Secretary Johnston felt that God was calling him to a different type of Christian service. As he travelled around the country on deputation work he realised that he loved to be out proclaiming the Gospel amongst the people, and so in September 1993 he resigned his position to begin training for the ministry of the Presbyterian Church in Union College, Belfast.

In a break from tradition, and taking into account the changing nature of the work and the increasing financial constraints upon it with the passing of the years, the person whom the Mission Board appointed as his successor did not come from within its existing staff, but was a man with a wealth of experience in business. George Ferguson was someone in whom a sincere Christian faith and passion for the souls of men and women and a lifetime of hands-on experience in church affairs and the world of commerce all combined to make him appear a sensible choice. At the time of his appointment he was Session Clerk of 2nd Newtownards Presbyterian Church and very heavily involved in the work of Christian Endeavour.

George began his work with the Mission having been accorded the more up-to-date title of Executive Secretary, and as with all those who had preceded him from William Maxwell down, both his spiritual integrity and his business acumen were to be thoroughly tested in the years ahead. He believed, though, that God had led him into that position and He had promised never to leave him or forsake him.

That, at least, was comforting.

When he had established a working relationship with all the local missionaries the new Executive Secretary set about expanding the operational base of the Mission. He had heard from some of those involved, of the 1988 campaign in Carnalbanagh, and from others and the mission records of the evangelistic missions conducted out in country churches by men like William Wylie and David Hamilton. These were ardent evangelists who had a overriding desire to see people won for the Master, and George Ferguson, having been possessed of a similar sort of vision, gradually made it known that his missionaries would be available to conduct missions in country areas, depending on availability.

This idea was welcomed by many of the rural ministers and their congregations. Not that there was anything wrong with their 'man' who had been preaching to them every week for years but it would, they thought, be nice to have some fiery young fellow from the city up to talk to them for a change!

Many missions were conducted outside the city from 1995 onwards, and in most of these people were led to faith in Christ and others who were lapsed church members began to attend regularly once more.

In March 2000 a team of three missionaries, Errol McCrory, David Surgeoner and Lloyd Watson began house-to-house visitation in the district around Drumhillery Presbyterian Church in County Armagh. They were preparing for a two-week Gospel campaign in the Church where George Ferguson had undertaken to do most of the preaching.

There were just fifty-nine families in the small country congregation and on the first Sunday night only about eighty people turned up at the meeting.

The men on the ground weren't discouraged, though. They were aware that this outreach had been preceded by much prayer. All they had to do, they knew, was work longer and pray harder.

One morning early in the mission they were visiting around a cluster of houses just opposite the Church, when they came across an elderly man clearing up around the flowerbeds in his front garden.

"We will help you to do that Mister," one of the missionaries offered. In a short space of time, and before he had even time to object, 'Mister's' big black bin bag was full of rotting leaves and other slippery, slimy half-rotten rubbish that had been left after the winter.

As they were about to leave the astonished man asked, "Who are you and why have you done this for me?"

"We are from the Church over there across the road," one of the men volunteered. "There are meetings on there every night of the week and we would like it if you could come along sometime."

"After all that you have done for me, I probably will drop over a night," he replied, very thankful that somebody had been prepared to help him.

He kept his promise, began to attend regularly, and during the second week accepted Jesus into his heart.

Both numbers and interest increased, and on the final Sunday night of the meetings almost three hundred people were packed into the relatively small church.

That night as the congregation was filing out, many of them sad that the mission had come to an end, a lady who had been singing in the choir every night, held George firmly by the hand.

"Mr. Ferguson," she said, " I have just discovered in this mission that although I have been attending this church and singing in the choir all my life, I am not ready to meet God. I don't want to stay behind now but would you please send somebody round to the farm tomorrow to talk to me."

"I certainly will," George promised, and he did.

When two of the younger men arrived at the farm next morning there was no response to a knock at the door. It was spring, it was a sheep farm, it was lambing time, and it was busy.

After some echoing calls around the farm the missionaries eventually found the lady, dressed for work, in a lambing shed.

It was quite a new experience for the two missionaries from the city, but in that shed, surrounded by bleating sheep and hours-old lambs, they had the joy of seeing that lady exercise simple faith in Christ.

And she was the eighth of the mission that the missionaries knew about.

Away across at the western edge of the Province the city missionaries had been invited to conduct a joint campaign with a number of evangelically minded churches in the Killen Community Centre in Castlederg, County Tyrone, in 2001.

Willie Cowan, Robin Fairbairn, Raymond Hume and Billy Mc Cullough visited around the area and some of the people of the district began to come along to the meetings. Four people, a lady and her daughter, and two other young men committed their lives to Christ. That was thrilling.

On the Friday of the one-week outreach Robin Fairbairn engaged a man in conversation at his door.

"Do you normally go to church?" Robin asked as they talked together.

"Aye, I go to a lot of churches," came the man's reply.

"Well then, why don't you come down to the Community Centre tonight. Some of the Churches around here have combined and are having some meetings there in the evenings," the missionary went on to inform him.

"I suppose I could," the man was cautiously non-committal. "If I don't get down tonight I'll maybe come on Sunday."

Friday night passed with no sign of him at the final weeknight meeting.

He had said, though, that he would 'maybe come on Sunday'.

The four missionaries prayed that he would, and he did.

At the close of the service on the Sunday evening the man went up and spoke to Willie Sayers, who had been the soloist that evening, and within a few minutes both men disappeared into a little side room.

Some time later they emerged and as they approached Robin Fairbairn, Willie said to the man who was standing, smiling, by his side, "Tell him what you have just done."

"I have given my life to Jesus," he replied in a simple confession of a newly found faith. He had come on Sunday, not only to the meeting, but also to the Saviour.

That mission in Castlederg had proved very worthwhile for at least five people had come to faith in Christ during the week.

The willingness of the City Mission to conduct campaigns and organise visitation programmes in various parts of the province gradually opened up a further window of opportunity for them. Their dedication to the work of the Lord and unashamed emphasis on evangelism led to the Mission being invited to supply speakers to vacant congregations. This in its turn had a two-fold positive effect. It allowed men whose main aim was to see people saved a chance to preach the Gospel, while also helping to create an awareness of the Mission and its work, in country areas.

Despite its increasing interest in and commitment to conducting services in different parts of the country, the City Mission never lost sight of the fact that its primary and extensive mission field was the streets and estates of Belfast.

Here, too, time had brought changes into both the social and moral environments in which the missionaries were working, making it more difficult to reach people with the message of heavenly love and eternal life.

The Loyalist feud saw much heartbreak amongst some of the people with whom the missionaries had worked. Families were driven from their homes in fear, often relocating at secret addresses.

Tom Gamble, who was missionary in Bellvue Street was surprised and disappointed when a family of five who had been regular in their attendance at Sunday School didn't appear for two weeks in a row. On calling around to the street where they had lived he found their home closed up and a neighbour informed him that 'they have moved'.

Some time later Tom received a letter thanking his wife Deborah and him for all they had done for the family, and saying how the children missed the Sunday School. No address was included but a simple paragraph explained the reason.

'I know I haven't included any address,' the appreciative mother wrote, 'as we are still wary of anyone finding out where we are, due to the circumstances that we are left under. Unfortunately, certain people would be glad of our address at the moment. We have had to move twice already…'

A number of families who came regularly to the Mayo Street Hall were also affected by this feud. One distraught mother had two sons, both living at home with her, and both on opposing sides in the dispute. This caused endless conflict in the home and distress for the mother. The missionary did what he could to help solve the situation, but without much success.

In August 2000, Tom was just starting the second week of his holiday when he received an urgent request to return home. A man who had once attended Mayo street Hall had been shot dead in the dispute and the family had requested that Tom conduct the funeral.

This was someone whom the missionary had known for many years and he found the whole situation difficult to cope with. However, he was supported by the prayers of his many Christian friends and his fellow-workers in the Mission. At the service he was enabled to use the opportunity to emphasise, with all the tact required in the circumstances but with appropriate earnestness also, the realities of the brevity of life, and the necessity of preparing to meet God after death.

Another incident, which demonstrated the nature of the problems facing the Christian worker in our present society, occurred across in the Kilburn Street Hall in the south west of the city.

J.J. was a bright little boy who loved coming along to the Children's meeting in the Hall. At a summer Five Day Club he showed great interest in the message and the leaders were praying for him that he would surrender his life to Christ.

As the week went on the little boy's mother, probably stricken by a guilty conscience, said to one of the leaders when she called to pick up her son, "I think I have said something very wrong to J.J."

"And what's that?" the leader enquired, puzzled.

"I have told him that I don't want him to become a Christian for if he does I will find it very difficult to continue with my present life-style, and I have no intention of giving it up," she confessed.

What a dilemma for a little boy!

As the work of God continued to progress in both city and country in the 90's a further challenge faced the Executive Secretary.

In some districts old Halls would need to be replaced and in at least one other a new building would have to be erected to accommodate an expanding work.

His business skills were about to be tested to the limit, in the service of his Divine Master, and the Belfast City Mission.

29

THE COWS THAT ATE THE ASTERS

Saturday September 5, 1992 was a notable day in the life of the Belfast City Mission for two different reasons. It was on that day that Professor D.A.D. Montgomery performed the opening ceremony at a Hall in Bloomfield Drive. This new building had been erected to replace the former Hall in East Bread Street, which, like so many in the previous half-century, had to be demolished to make way for a modern development. A new shopping centre at Connswater was scheduled to be built over the site of the former Hall.

Sadly that was to be Dr. Montgomery's last official function on behalf of the Mission for it was then that he announced that he was standing down from the office of President which he had upheld with honour for almost twenty years.

Mr. Desmond Shaw was then invited to become President of the Belfast City Mission and Mr. David Surgeoner, who had been missionary in East Bread Street for six years, began work in the new Hall in Bloomfield Avenue. Although he and his helpers in the Hall had arranged a full programme of meetings for the week, including a Mother and Toddlers Group and a Youth club, he was soon to realise that it was going to be an uphill struggle to persuade the residents from round about to come in.

Calling at a home one afternoon, the missionary asked a young woman what she most desired out of life.

"I don't know," was her curt reply. "But what I do know is that I don't want to waste any more of it talking to you!"

It would be inclined to put one off, but David wasn't that easily discouraged. He persevered with the work in Bloomfield Avenue and saw a number led to faith in Christ.

Something which had only happened a few times in all the years of the Mission occurred again in October 1994. The Belfast City Mission was given the gift of a Hall on the understanding that they would keep it open as a Gospel witness in the district.

Herbert Martin and his father before him had run an independent Mission Hall in the Woodvale district of the city for eighty years. When Mr. Martin found it impossible to carry on the work there because of failing health and the absence of anyone to take over from him he arranged for the Hall to be transferred into the charge of the City Mission.

This was good.

Established Halls in densely populated districts didn't always come that easily.

Adrian Adger was appointed as missionary to the district and as he began a programme of door-to-door visitation people began to come back to the Hall and the work was built up once more.

Shortly after his appointment, George Ferguson realised that something would have to be done, and soon, to alleviate the accommodation problems that Raymond Hume was experiencing with his work in Fairview Road, in Ballyduff on the northern edge of the city.

Raymond had been appointed missionary to the district in 1988 and had begun by calling from door to door in the area, introducing himself, and where possible the good news of the Gospel.

It was heard at first, but one gleam began to show on a very distant horizon when a Christian couple that he had met in the course of his daily visitations invited him to start a prayer group in their home. Knowing that revivals had begun from prayer meetings in the past, Raymond was pleased to accept the offer and on the first night just the four predictables turned up. They were the host and hostess and the missionary and his wife. Undeterred, they prayed and determined to tell others of their little prayer meeting. The next week the numbers had doubled. There were eight present!

As news spread amongst the local community of the prayer meeting each week in the home, others came along, and soon it was decided that the time had come to reach out to the district with the Gospel.

The City Mission began to search for premises in which Raymond could begin an outreach work, and hired a small room above a shop in Woodford, a housing development in the Ballyduff district.

Although the room was small it served to allow the Mission to establish an identity in the district and Sunday evening and mid-week services commenced. It was amongst children and young people, though, that the work really developed. A Sunday School and then a mid-week Children's meeting were commenced. Large numbers of enthusiastic children and a few regular teenagers attending those activities motivated Raymond and a number of loyal helpers to weld another link into the chain attaching their little group above the shop to the local people who shopped in it.

They would set up a Girls Brigade Company.

This proved to be an immediate hit with a number of the girls of the district and their parents. So many came that the little room proved far too small to accommodate the junior company within six months. The leaders could just about manage to cram all the girls into the room but there certainly wasn't any spare space for physical or creative activity! Thus the Community Centre, which was not available in the evenings, was hired on a weekday afternoon after school hours, and the junior company began to meet there, and grow even bigger. The senior group, which was not so large, just about managed to carry on in the room above the shop in Woodford.

God blessed this work. Girls were led to Christ in the Girls Brigade and still the work continued to advance in all its aspects.

The Sunday School and Children's meeting had both begun to outgrow the existing room and the Girls Brigade had done so long since. More spacious accommodation was urgently needed.

Hence it fell as one of the first tasks facing George in his position as Executive Secretary to address the problem of finding, or building, somewhere new to allow the work which had been established in the Ballyduff area to expand even more.

He entered into negotiations with the Housing Executive for a piece of land which they had released for sale on Fairview Road. This was eventually procured at an agreed price and the first hurdle had been overcome. God had led them to an ideally placed site, right in the heart of the community. The next problem was one of finance.

When an architect had been asked to draw up a plan for a Hall large enough to cater for all the varied activities of the expanding group it was discovered that such a building would probably cost in excess of one hundred thousand pounds.

This sounded a colossal amount of money to some members of the Mission Board but their new secretary gently reminded a few of them that he believed that they served an omnipotent God who could supply all the needs of His servants. If they would commit the matter to the Lord, and it was in His will, He would meet their need.

Plans were made to proceed with a building programme, using funds available, and everyone involved prayed particularly that God would meet help them meet the financial commitment of the new Hall that was soon to be constructed in Fairview Road.

It appeared like just another busy day in the Mission office when George Ferguson received a call from a firm of solicitors in a provincial town. "Mr. Ferguson," the lady said, "I have been asked to ring and tell you that the Belfast City Mission is going to receive a bequest from an estate that we are handling. Perhaps you could call at the office at your convenience and we can give you the details."

As he drove to an appointment with the solicitors the next day, the Secretary wondered how much the bequest would be for. Kind benefactors in the past had left gifts of two and five thousand pounds to the Mission. A really generous legacy would have been ten thousand. Could he even dare hope for something like that? Surely a legacy of that nature would prove to all that God was stamping His seal of approval on the Fairview Road project.

God didn't deal in half measures, though.

When he found out the size of the bequest George Ferguson was absolutely flabbergasted. It was for one hundred and forty thousand pounds, a sum which would probably prove sufficient to build and furnish the new Hall about to be built on Fairview Road.

The Board of the Mission had reinforced for them, something they already knew but needed to have re-emphasised occasionally. It was an exciting discovery that Paul, in the Bible, had made in his lifetime. God is able to carry out His purpose and do super-abundantly, infinitely beyond all that we can ask for, or even imagine.

Assured that God had been guiding in every aspect of the work in the district the Board proceeded with the building programme and a new Hall was erected on the site in Fairview Road. This Hall was declared open, on September 22, 1995 by Mrs. Daisy Buick and her husband, Rev. Jackson Buick, the district Superintendent, addressed the capacity congregation.

God had done wonderful things in the room above the shop in Woodford and had provided for a new facility in Fairview Road. Raymond Hume and his increasing band of dedicated assistants looked forward to His continued blessing in the new building in the days ahead.

Having proved the goodness and guidance of God in the provision of the Fairview Road Hall the directors of the City Mission found themselves confronted with another similar accommodation situation.

The old, temporary wooden hall in Glencairn had outlived its usefulness. It was in need of repair, but more crucially it was no longer big enough to cope with the increasing numbers of young people who were coming along to its youth activities. Many of those associated with the Mission, both across the city and the province, joined George Lunn the missionary, and the Christians in the district in earnest prayer about the matter.

And again God, in His bounty, stepped in to meet the need in a most remarkable way.

On September 3, 1997, the Executive Secretary received a letter from another firm of solicitors informing him that they were acting in the administration of an estate of a lady who had died a few weeks earlier. This person had bequeathed one quarter of the residue of her estate to the Belfast City Mission, and the estate included a valuable piece of land.

Having searched in vain through the Mission's records to find any trace of this benefactor George Ferguson was completely bamboozled.

Why, he wondered, would someone, of whom nobody at the Mission had ever heard, want to leave money to them? He went to see the solicitors to see if they could shed any further light on the matter, and was told an astonishing story.

The lady in question had lived in a bungalow which had been built on the edge of the land she owned. She was a keen gardener and the beautiful flower borders around the bungalow were her pride and joy.

Not having any use for the surrounding land, however, she had leased it to a local farmer for grazing, and in her will had left it to him.

One day a number of the farmer's cows strayed too close to the green-fingered lady's garden fence, and half-a-dozen or so of them spotted some lush green vegetation on the other side. The cows then proceeded to do what any curious cow would do in the circumstances.

They stretched over and helped themselves!

In a short space of time a once brightly coloured herbaceous border had been decimated. Asters and anemones, dahlias and delphiniums, phlox and fuchsias had all been reduced to a standard height of nine inches above the ground!

The lady was furious!

She immediately telephoned the solicitors and arranged a meeting with them to have her will amended. The farmer lost out but it was at that stage that Belfast City Mission became a beneficiary. How, or from whom she had heard of them, though, still remained a mystery!

When the land was sold and the estate wound up Belfast City Mission received a legacy of two hundred and fifty thousand pounds, enough to build a large Hall equipped to twenty-first century standards, from a lady nobody knew!

The new hall, which was built on the site of the old temporary structure, was opened in November 2000. Now the City Mission had a suitable, permanent base from which to reach out to the people of Glencairn.

Telling someone, on that day, of how God had provided for the needs of the building George Ferguson quoted the words of William Cowper's hymn,

'God moves in a mysterious way,

 His wonders to perform...'

It's true. He does.

The Belfast City Mission has proved that more than once in its history in His service.

30

TWO THOUSAND AND TWO

With the dawn of the twenty-first century and its endless emphasis on the streamlining of super services for smarter living the City Mission began to examine further ways in which it could make an appreciable impact for God amongst the citizens, and on the streets, of Belfast.

In an ultra-modern, fast-lane, mobile phone society the old problems remained. People were determined to 'live it up', whatever the cost, and the thought of God, or death, or eternity never seemed to cross their minds. Widespread overt drunkenness had been replaced by widespread covert drug addiction. Fewer children than ever were attending Sunday School. Surveys showed that up to seventy per cent of all the young people in the city had no contact whatsoever with a place of worship.

What was to be done?

How could these problems be addressed?

The Executive Secretary, George Ferguson, and his assistant, Robin Fairbairn, began to think about these matters and decided, after prayerful consideration, to attempt to introduce a ministry to the Primary Schools in the city. If the children weren't coming to the churches and Mission Halls as they once did, then they would try to go out to them, where they had to be.

How, though, did they go about initiating such a venture?

Robin had been speaking in the morning assembly in Nettlefield Primary School on a regular basis for a few years and George and he asked the Principal there, Mr. David Todd, and other Christians they knew, for advice. After a further period of prayerful consultation they came to the conclusion that the best approach would be to write to Primary Schools within the city boundary. In their letter they offered the services of someone to teach the pupils a Bible lesson in the morning assembly on a one-off or regular, once-a-term basis. They then followed the letter up with a telephone call to the Schools a few weeks later.

The response was very encouraging.

Robin Fairbairn assumed responsibility for most of this work and visits twenty Schools per term every term, armed with his Bible and visual aids of different kinds. In this way hundreds of children who may otherwise never hear of Jesus and His love are being introduced, in a professional manner, to the One who said, "Allow the little children to come to Me and don't try to stop them, for of such is the kingdom of God."

In addition to the excellent work being done for God in the Mission Halls, some of which had been forced to relocate amongst the large population concentrations on the outskirts of the city, the Mission realised that one of the busiest human thoroughfares of the city still remained relatively untouched by its missionaries.

It was the city centre.

The return to a measure of peace in the province and the growth of modern office blocks and shopping malls in downtown Belfast had seen the city centre become a throbbing mass of cosmopolitan life once again. It was a neutral environment and thus an ideal mission field for it was populated by all kinds of people. There were business executives and office workers, tourists and students, day- trippers and night sleepers, and every single one of them needed to hear the Gospel

In an effort to reach out to these people the Belfast City Mission appointed John Miskelly to contact them with the good news of Jesus

Christ and Willie Cowan succeeded John as missionary to the city centre in 1999. This was a new concept for the Mission, for in John and then Willie they had missionaries with a district but no Hall in which to hold meetings, or for which to be responsible.

Willie Cowan loved the Lord and he loved this work. He left home every morning stocked up with Bibles and Christian literature and walked around speaking to people where he found them, about the Saviour. This could be in a railway station, or at a bus stop, up near the University or down along Royal Avenue

It worked. As the missionary tramped the streets of his bustling mission field, engaging people in conversation, he found some dissatisfied souls and within a few months of his appointment he had led a man who had been sitting drinking on a seat outside the City Hall, to Christ. This man told Willie that when he was a boy of sixteen he had attended open-airs and Gospel meetings but he had been 'away from all of that' for forty years. Now, like the prodigal, he had 'come home', and Willie left him, after a long session, happy to begin a new life as a Christian.

This man was only one of more than thirty people that Willie had seen led to faith in Christ in the first two and a half years of his ministry, but such people presented him with a certain concern. Although he was happy that they had been converted the chances were that he would never see them again. He had no base in which to meet them.

This raised another thought in his mind. If he only had somewhere accessible to his city centre 'patch' to which he could invite seemingly interested enquirers it would help him to have more fruitful conversations with them. Two years on the streets had reminded Willie that the sun didn't always shine in Belfast, and on wet or windy, frosty or foggy afternoons, people weren't all that keen to stand around.

He shared these thoughts with the Secretary who had been considering the feasibility of opening up some kind of a city centre station for Willie and his work. Everyone, from the President, through to the new Honorary Secretary, Rev. Jackson Buick, who had just succeeded Dr. John Girvan in the post, and the Board members and all the serving missionaries agreed that a neutral unit of some sort should be established without delay. This outpost would, all who knew of the proposal stressed, have to be something far removed from the church or mission hall image. The people Willie was working with weren't 'churchy' types.

A café would be ideal.

When the go-ahead to search for a suitable property was given the business skills of the Executive Secretary came into play again. Estate agents were contacted, expert advice was sought, all kinds of available properties were visited, and eventually a vacant shop on Dublin Road was leased in June 2002.

This was an answer to prayer once more.

God had led the men who were endeavouring to set up a base for Christian work in the city centre to a suitable unit on one of its busiest thoroughfares!

The shop unit they had rented was just a rundown shell, however. Before it opened as a café or coffee shop or whatever it would have to be refurbished and then furnished.

Although the task looked daunting it proved no problem to a Heavenly Father with a family of talented children.

When the news of this new venture of faith began to spread amongst the Presbyterian Churches and City Mission Halls in Belfast, workmen, materials and equipment seemed to arrive in a steady stream on the pavement outside 93 Dublin Road.

Tradesmen of all kinds offered their specialist skills free of charge.

A restaurant that was closing down offered the Mission its tables and chairs, crockery and cutlery for the Searcher's Café.

Someone supplied a C.D. player and another enough carpet to cover the floors and the services of a carpet-fitter to lay it!

An upstairs room was furnished as a quiet room, or sanctuary. This was a place apart from the clamour and chatter of the café down below, a tranquil spot where seeking people could be counselled, well away from the clank of cups and saucers and the whirr of coffee-making machines.

After a summer of feverish activity the outreach Café opened its doors to the passing public on Tuesday, August 13, 2002. There was no prolonged opening ceremony in this case, nobody in a flowery hat to cut a ribbon, or no minister to preach for half-an-hour.

This was an outreach of a novel kind, but within weeks of its opening it had justified its existence in spiritual terms.

One of the first people to trust Christ in the café was a lady from the Donegall Pass district of the city, not far away. She was passing and Willie Cowan offered her a booklet and began to speak to her about salvation. When he heard that she was very confused and 'didn't know what to believe for all sorts of people had been calling at her door telling her about different religions' the missionary invited her to come into the café and talk the matter over.

Within an hour the missionary had pointed that 'confused' lady to Christ and on keeping in contact with her discovered that she had begun to attend the meetings in the Mission Hall in Sandy Row.

In early October 2002, Willie spoke to a young woman in the street outside the café one day at lunchtime. The woman worked farther along the Dublin Road and was out for a walk when Willie met her.

As they talked the missionary heard a sad story, but one of a kind that he had heard from others on different occasions before.

"I became a Christian when I was a young girl," the smart young lady told him, "but then I went across to work in England and discovered vodka. I began drinking and started to go out to parties nearly every night. Now I am away from God, and all mixed up." She paused before going on, "And my father is never off my back about my lifestyle."

Willie told her that she should come back to God, and He would welcome her as an erring, straying sheep returning to the fold of His love.

It was time for the employee to return to her work, but the only response she would make to Willie's wise counsel was a half-hearted, "I might. I'll see."

Then, as though she had been embarrassed by her revelations to a complete stranger, she added before hurrying off, "Anyway, I don't know why I have told you all of this."

Perhaps she didn't know why she had opened her heart to the sympathetic missionary, but he did. Willie Cowan and the other missionaries began to pray for her.

Just over a week later the woman appeared in the café one day, looking for Willie.

"I want to tell you,' she said, 'that by a strange chance Mr. Ferguson from your Mission was preaching in our church last Sunday, and I have decided to get myself sorted out, whatever it costs. What should I do?"

After talking to her for some time Willie advised her to go home and begin reading her Bible and praying again and God would speak to her.

A few days later the young lady called in again and told the missionary, "I have done what you said and God has spoken to me through His word. I have sorted myself out towards God and I am going to go on and live for Him from now on."

It had been worthwhile opening the Searcher's Café even if it was only to make this contact.

And still the work continued.

When distributing appropriate literature in the University area of the city Willie met a young student from Crossmaglen in the south of the province.

"Have you heard the good news?" Willie asked him by way of introduction.

"No, I haven't. What's that?" the fellow asked, somewhat bemused.

"It's that God loved the world and that His Son, Jesus Christ came to earth to die on a Cross to take away the sin of all who will trust in Him," the street-walking missionary informed him. Having captured his attention Willie then proceeded to tell him of God's wonderful plan for the salvation of mankind.

"You know," the student responded thoughtfully when Willie had finished his pithy word of witness, "I never heard that in my life before."

He had never heard the Gospel message in his life before.

It was interesting that the first person to tell him the marvellous story, was William Cowan, a man from Lisburn.

One hundred and seventy five years earlier another Lisburn man, William Cochrane, had arrived in the town of Belfast with the sole intent of bringing the same message to people with exactly the same spiritual needs, but who lived in a very different kind of society.

The Mission has made vast strides from then.

In 1827 William Cochrane was the Town Mission's sole agent.

Now the Belfast City Mission has twenty-four full-time missionaries.

In 1827 the agent had to proclaim the message in a rented 'station'.

Now the Belfast City Mission owns and maintains twenty Mission halls, many of them equipped to the very highest standards, across the city, as well as an outreach café and a charity shop.

In 1827 the total income handled by the Mission was William Cochrane's annual salary and the rental of his preaching 'station'.

In 2002 it was almost half-a-million pounds.

Mere facts and figures cannot even attempt to measure the worth of the City Mission to the city of Belfast, however.

It is only when the books are balanced in heaven that its true value will be revealed.

Hundreds of spiritually inspired men and women down the years have visited in homes bringing with them a simple blend of scriptural truth and physical support. They have preached in halls and in the open air. They have conducted funerals, taught in Sunday Schools, and led youth organisations, all with the same object in view. That was to see people led to Christ.

It wasn't always easy but God blessed their dedicated efforts in a marvellous way. Thousands were saved as a result of their labours.

The waves of blessing that have begun in Belfast have caused ripples all around the world. Many of those who came to the Saviour, possibly as children, in Canton Street or Kimberly Street, Ballybeen or Ballysillan, have lived, or are now living for their Lord, not only in Belfast and Northern Ireland but in many other lands as well.

The work hasn't finished yet, either.

The present Board and it hard-working band of godly missionaries will carry it on as God will guide them, in the years to come.

It is to Him, and Him alone that they would render the praise for all that is past.

And it is to Him alone that they look for all that's to come.

BELFAST CITY MISSION

~ Presidents ~

Mr. Thomas Sinclair	1893 – 1913
Mr. Thomas Mc Bride	1913 – 1922
Mr. James G. Crawford	1922 – 1937
Mr. F. J. Holland	1937 – 1961
Mr. T. H. Jemphrey	1961 – 1965
Mr. J. D. Bailie	1965 – 1973
Dr. D. A. D. Montgomery	1973 – 1992
Mr. Desmond J. Shaw	1992 –

~ Secretaries ~

Mr. William Maxwell	1889 – 1913
Mr. Francis Mulligan	1913 – 1943
Mr. William Wylie	1943 – 1960
Mr. David Hamilton	1960 – 1983
Mr. William Cooke	1983 – 1990
Mr. Johnston Lambe	1990 – 1993
Mr. George Ferguson	1993 –

OTHER BOOKS BY THE SAME AUTHOR

MY FATHER'S HAND

THIS IS FOR REAL

JUST THE WAY I AM

SOME PARTY IN HEAVEN

FIRST CITIZEN SMYTH

SOMETHING WORTH LIVING FOR

HOW SWEET THE SOUND

AS OUR HEADS ARE BOWED

ONLY THE BEST WILL DO

A BRUISED REED

BACK FROM THE BRINK

OUT OF THE MAZE

THE TANGLED LAMB

SOLDIER, SAILOR, LIVE OR DIE

I BELIEVE GOD

PAINTING THE TOWN RED